I WANT the Cross!

I WANT the Cross!

LIVING A RADICAL FAITH

SEAN DUNN

Fleming H. Revell
A Division of Baker Book House Co
Grand Rapids, Michigan 49516

Published by Fleming H. Revell
a division of Baker Book House Company
P.O. Box 6287, Grand Rapids, MI 49516-6287

Printed in the United States of America

Library of Congress Cataloging-in-Publication Data

Dunn, Sean, 1968–
    I want the cross! : living a radical faith / Sean Dunn.
        p.   cm.
    ISBN 0-8007-5740-8 (paper)
    1. Christian teenagers—Religious life. I. Title.
    BV4531.3.D86 2001
    248.8'3—dc21   00-047069

Scripture quotations are from the HOLY BIBLE, NEW INTERNATIONAL VERSION®. NIV®. Copyright © 1973, 1978, 1984 by International Bible Society. Used by permission of Zondervan Publishing House. All rights reserved.

The song "I Lay It before You" in chapter 4 is © 1990 by Chris Hansler and is used by permission.

For current information about all releases from Baker Book House, visit our web site:

http://www.bakerbooks.com

Contents

I Want the Cross!

I can still remember the emotion surrounding that evening. The excitement and anticipation leading up to that point had been building for two days. Finally, in a dramatic moment, I stood and shouted along with several hundred teenagers, "I want the cross!"

What a Rush

Our journey through three states in a bus that could barely reach the speed limit had taken us three days. When we arrived in Southern California, we spent a few days taking in the scenery, checking out the beach, shopping, and going to Disneyland, but then the real attraction began. My youth group (about forty of us) had taken this excursion in the summer of 1985 to attend a youth convention in Tajunga, California. We were excited about the prospect of gathering with teenagers from all over the country who wanted to grow closer to God.

As the convention began, the worship team led us in anthems of praise. Even the people from our group who normally did not participate in song services lifted their voices in worship. Before the speaker began his talk, we were already experiencing the presence of God, and it was captivating. It was with great expectation that we awaited what was going to take place.

Rich Wilkerson was the speaker. His humor intrigued us, but his messages were the most riveting. That week-end Rich spoke to us three times. Each time was meaningful and powerful, but I will never forget the final challenge he gave us.

Rich began his message that night by painting a picture of what it means to follow Christ as a disciple. He encouraged us to count the cost, to consider the consequences, and then to make a conscious decision to choose Jesus. After several minutes of solidifying his points, he read Luke 9:23: "Then he said to them all: 'If anyone would come after me, he must deny himself and take up his cross daily and follow me.'"

As he brought his message to a close that night, I felt as though I was about to burst. I could feel the presence of the Lord, and I could clearly hear him speaking to me. I knew the Lord was calling me to a deeper, more committed walk with him. What had started as a group trip was quickly becoming an individual encounter with the Lord.

With each moment, my heart began to beat harder and faster. As my pulse raced, I was silently urging Rich on. I had already made up my mind that I needed to respond, and I wanted to do it then and there. As Rich gave instructions for the altar time, I waited anxiously and nervously for my chance to confirm my choice to be a disciple. Rich explained that he did not want this moment to be like so many before. He wanted us to make conscious choices to pursue God, not emotional decisions. He didn't want us to respond with our friends or our youth groups; he wanted us to make sure we were responding to God for the right reasons. Continuing, he told us, "When you feel you are ready to respond to the Lord, I want you to stand up and shout at the top of your lungs, 'I want the cross!'"

With keyboards playing in the background, Rich led us in a simple prayer. As soon as the amen was said, the musician stopped playing and silence filled the room. The quietness only intensified the beating of my heart, which by now was pounding like a hammer in my chest. I was not conscious of anything happening around me. I was counting the cost. Quietly, I searched my heart one more time. I wanted Jesus. I was ready. I wanted to go all the way.

Jumping out of my seat and thrusting both hands into the air, I shouted, "I want the cross!" The auditorium was filling with voices declaring the same thing. The phrase rang out as one by one my peers shouted those words. The tone in each voice was different, but the sincerity that backed each passionate cry was the same.

That night many people came to Christ, ready, willing, and desiring to follow him no matter what the cost.

Reality Check

The trip didn't last long. In just over twenty-four hours we were on our way back home. Our group had settled into the bus, and most of the teens were sleeping. A few were listening to music on their headphones; some were talking in the back. I was sitting alone, roaming through the memories of the convention.

A little more than a day had passed, and I was already beginning to question what had taken place at the last service. I wasn't beginning to doubt God and what he had done or said. I was soul-searching, wondering if I could ever live up to the commitments I had made.

That weekend was not the first time I had encountered the Lord, nor was it the first time I had emotionally responded to him. Many times during my teenage years I had come to an altar to declare boldly before God and my friends that I was going to be different. It seemed as though at every camp, youth rally, and convention I had attended, I had surrendered to the tug in my heart. The only problem was that my past had proven to me that I had not been able to live up to my promises.

As I sat on the bus, with forty people who were my friends around me, I was alone. I wasn't even home yet, but I was already declaring myself defeated. *I will never be able to be who I want to be and to walk with God boldly like I want.* I sat there in the silent bus, convincing myself that I would never be able to overcome my weaknesses.

Although my pity party seemed to last for hours, I now realize that it was pretty short-lived. Within twenty or thirty minutes, something crashed my party. I could say that it was God, but to be totally honest, I am not sure

what it was. It might have been my self-confidence return-
ing or logic that had escaped me, but something began to
change in my heart that day.

Sitting there on a vinyl seat in an old beat-up bus, a part
of me that I had not seen in a while came to visit. My determination and my willingness to fight for what I wanted
showed up. Courage to try again entered my body and
consumed my thoughts—slowly at first, then with the
urgency and power of a raging river. I began to quietly give
myself a pep talk, and with each passing moment, I grew
more convinced that I could make it. I had to make it. I
wasn't willing to settle for anything less this time.

What a Day

That day, that very hour, my life changed. I will never
be certain what took place in my heart. All I know is that
my burning desire to overcome my own doubt pushed me
into a place where I have never fallen away from God. That
is not to say I have always felt as "on fire" for God as I did
at that youth service, but in that moment I embraced the
Lord so tightly that I have never allowed myself to slip
away from him.

As you read my story, I am sure you could see some sim-
ilarities with yourself. Most young people are just like I
was back then. They are fed up with their past failures, and
they are frustrated that they can't live up to their commitments. Their roller-coaster spiritual life is getting tir-
ing, and they want some consistency.

The purpose of this book is to help you get to where you
want to be. The principles laid out in these pages may seem
basic at times, but they are true. When taken and applied

to your life, they will braid you together with the Lord in a way that will give you strength, hope, courage, and most of all stability. My prayer for you is that as you read this book, you will apply each chapter to your life. If you do, your journey with the Lord will become very exciting.

Principles to Ponder and Practice

- Can you relate to the feelings and fears I experienced on that bus? When was the last time you felt that way?
- Have you ever failed God? When and how?
- Are you ready to start anew and overcome previous failures?

Let God Build You

I love reading about King David. If I were to choose a biblical hero apart from Christ, I would have to choose David. He did some great things for God and was a great man. I have always admired him for these traits.

King David Was a Valiant Warrior

One of the things I respect and admire about David is the courage and confidence he exuded when facing frightening odds. As a young man, he took on a nine-foot giant and knew that he couldn't lose. Carrying just a rock and a piece of cloth, he went up against Goliath, and with a confidence that bordered on arrogance, he told the giant that he was going to feed his flesh to the birds of the air. David won the battle with his faith before the rock ever left the sling.

David's most memorable battle was against Goliath, but it was not his only victory. History records many other events that prove David's success as a warrior on the battlefield.

King David Was a Visible Worshiper

One of the things that defined David was his visible worship of the Lord. Uninhibited by what others thought, David worshiped like few others before or after him. The worship lyrics recorded in the Book of Psalms point to his heart for the Lord, represented in intimate praise and communication.

David not only worshiped when times were good, he also kept his focus when times were not good. The Bible says that David worshiped with "all of his might." He held nothing back. His spirit, soul, and body participated when he worshiped. When his wife became embarrassed and rebuked him, he did not defend his image. He declared that he would lose himself even more in worship.

When I need an example of what it means to worship the Lord, I think of David. He challenges me to neglect my reputation and become lost in worship.

King David Was a Great King

David became the standard by which the other kings of Israel were judged. He ruled wisely and was obedient to the will of God in his reign. David made mistakes, but when you boil it down, the favor of God rested on David's administration. Even in the midst of his moral failures, he responded promptly and correctly to the Lord's conviction.

If I did as well at my job as David did at his, I would be pleased. If God graced me with the same favor as he did the second king of Israel, I would be doing well.

King David Was a Man after God's Heart

One of the greatest commendations ever given to a man was when Jehovah God declared that David was a man after his own heart. That statement is packed with significance. God declared that David had found favor with the heart of God. God was pleased with him. This statement also contains an indication of David's posture toward God. David was "after" God's heart. He was pursuing God, and God rewarded him.

Like David, I want to be a man after God's heart. It is important to me that I pursue God with everything I am. I believe that when I do so, I win his favor.

Where Was David Built?

When I think of David, I am reminded of the things he did and what he accomplished. His reputation was built on and around events in his life and things he did. One day, while thinking about David and intentionally trying to learn from his example, I asked the question, "Where was he built?"

I am convinced that nothing in God's plan is an accident. God did not stumble upon a need and randomly select someone who was close to the action to represent him. He planned ahead and built a man to champion his causes and defend his honor. David was God's man by design. However, I do not believe that David was born any different from you or me. God crafted him specifically for the task.

So where was he built? Was he built in the pressure of the palace or the stress of the battlefield? Was he molded for greatness in the public eye? No, he was shaped, sculpted, and prepared in quiet moments of solitude.

God Built David in Private to Use Him in Public

Peeking into the future, God determined what he was going to need to accomplish his purpose. God knew there would be a need for a valiant warrior, a visible worshiper, a great king, and a man after his heart. So he went about the task of building such a person.

For some reason, God's attention rested on David. He saw in him the potential to lead God's people in victory and by example. However, it was just potential . . . until God began to build David for his purposes.

God came to David and whispered in his ear, "Can I build you?" Not seeing the picture the way God did, the shepherd asked, "How and for what?" God's response came, "I will not tell you for what. I have a purpose for your life, but you will not know it immediately. However, I promise to watch over you and work for your good in the situations you face. You will be pleased with what you become." God continued, "As for how I will build you, I will sculpt you in private. When you are alone and recognize that I am there with you, I will begin to teach you. I will share my heart with you, and I will captivate your heart. In secret places, I will build you for greatness."

David's response was quick in coming. "Yes, I want you to build me. There is nothing that I want more than to spend time alone with you. I want to know your heart, and I want you to make me who you need me to be."

From that moment on, David, the shepherd boy, began a relationship with God like few others have known. While watching his sheep, he focused on God, and the communication they exchanged was intimate and intense. In those moments, David was being built. His faith was being strengthened. His leadership skills were being honed. Maturity and integrity were growing exponentially in his life.

For years, whenever David was alone, he realized it was an opportunity for God to come and befriend him. Every time God was invited, the Lord shaped David for greatness and for a purpose. The Master Builder was preparing David to face giants, to worship without shame, to lead a nation, and to represent his heart for generations to come.

The Principle Still Applies Today

God knows the future and what he needs. He will not be caught off guard when an opportunity arises. He knows what is coming, and he is in the process of building people to represent him as he builds his kingdom.

However, a problem exists today. Many people whom God wants to use are not willing to allow God to prepare them for the tasks that exist in the future. At times in the past, God asked them if they were willing to be built. He promised them fulfillment and purpose for their lives. But they did not like the process.

People in the world today long to do great things for God in the public arena, but they are not willing to be built in private. The world has a limited number of great leaders today because people have not been willing to draw

17

away into a quiet place with God. People who worship the Lord with all their might are few in number because people haven't spent time alone with God. Few people truly understand God's heart because they have not been trained in solitude.

A large number of people want to be used by God. They want to do public things that would bring the Lord recognition and honor. They would love to bring godly change into an ungodly world, but they skipped the preparation process. They missed the private building sessions with God.

If you want your life to count for God, you are going to have to learn to love being alone, because only when you are alone can God really prepare you for the task he has planned for you.

The Role of Solitude

The first time we meet David in Scripture, he is not fighting a battle or leading worship before a large congregation. He is tending sheep. He is in solitude.

The Spirit of the Lord has left King Saul, and the Lord has told Samuel to anoint the next king, one of the sons of Jesse. God has told Samuel where to find him—in Bethlehem. Word reaches Jesse and his sons that the man of God is coming to have a meal with them. Excitement stirs as the family talks about the purpose of Samuel's visit. However, one item of family business needs to be taken care of before Samuel arrives. Who is going to watch the family's flock of sheep? David is assigned the task.

I used to think that Jesse sent his youngest son out to look after the sheep because he saw David as insignificant. I thought it was demeaning for David to be left out of the family festivities. My mentality on the subject has changed, however. I wonder if David actually volunteered for the assignment.

I think David loved being alone, because in those moments he had an audience with God. Instead of longing to attend the feast with the prophet of God, David wanted to be in a place of solitude where he could spend time with God himself. I used to think David's solitary confinement was for the purpose of punishment initiated by his father. Now I believe that his moments alone, voluntarily taken, were for the purpose of preparation. People who are after God's heart volunteer to draw away from the crowd so they can spend time with the Lord.

Our society is desperately lacking people who have been built to bring about change. The reason is that people in our culture do not respond correctly when God asks, "Can I build you?" Instead of embracing the concept that God wants to shape and mold us, we reject it because it involves solitude. We do not like being alone in our society, and therefore, we fail to allow God to build us.

There are only three things you can do with solitude.

1. You can hate it. When God calls people to draw away with him, several refuse because they hate being alone. Rather than running into a quiet place, they seek out any distraction they can find to the quiet. They turn on the television, call a friend on the phone, or get on the Internet. Instead of staying home with God, they run out with friends; any friends will do as long as they do not have to stay home alone.

2. You can abuse it. Instead of hating solitude and avoiding it, some people actually abuse it. Time alone is a mechanism that God instituted to build us and shape us into men and women of God, yet many use their time alone to

accomplish just the opposite. Some people take moments of solitude and do things that steal from their destiny rather than help them build it. Instead of walking out of quiet moments more like Christ, they walk out more immoral. *What you set your affections on when you are alone will one day dominate your life when you are in public.* There will come a day when the things that are done behind closed doors will explode into the public eye. If you set your affections on Jesus Christ when you are alone, he will dominate your life when you are in public. However, if you set your affections on immorality, perversity, dishonesty, or ungodly schemes when you are alone, those things will dominate your life in public. There is a direct correlation between your moments of solitude and the type of person you will become in the public eye.

3. You can embrace it. Many people hate solitude; some abuse it. If you want to be a man or a woman who knows God and will be used by God to accomplish his purposes, you must learn to embrace solitude and make it a priority in your life. You must intentionally carve out time to be alone with God. Make appointments with him and do not break them. Time that you spend alone with him is the very lifeblood of your relationship.

What Has God Chosen You For?

God has already looked into the future, and he has determined what he needs you to be. You may have the opportunity to be a great businessman who will influence the corporate world. God may be shaping you to be an entertainer or an athlete. Perhaps God is preparing you to be a missionary, a pastor, or a Sunday school teacher. Maybe God wants to mold you into a godly spouse who raises godly children. Whatever God's purposes for your life are, they are important in his scheme of things. He is counting on you to let him build you.

There may be a nation with your name on it. Perhaps God is building you in private so that when he releases you in public, you can bring the gospel to the people. There may be a youth group that needs you. Maybe a community somewhere is praying for a godly mayor. There is much riding on your response to God when he asks if he can build you.

When David was born, he was full of potential. His response to solitude, however, turned that potential into promise. The same can be said of you.

Principles to Ponder and Practice

- In this chapter we talked about how King David was a valiant warrior, a visible worshiper, a great king, and a man after God's heart. Which one of these four attributes challenges you the most? What are you going to do to develop these attributes more in your life?

- What has been your response to solitude in the past? Have you avoided it, abused it, or embraced it?

- God is asking if he can build you. What is your response going to be? What are the benefits of responding correctly to his call to solitude? What will it cost you?

- On what have you been setting your affections? Is it something you would want to dominate your life in public?

Practice His Presence

Practice His Presence

"Practice makes perfect" is a phrase that was ingrained in me when I was growing up. At a young age, I discovered I liked sports. I did not just enjoy playing them, however. I wanted to be good. Many times it was not the competition with others that made me want to excel but the desire I had to keep improving and to do my best.

As a result, I began practicing on a regular basis. Although I played many sports and spent many hours working on each one, basketball was my favorite. Early in my school career, I developed a routine that I kept most days for years. On school days I would get up early enough to spend thirty minutes shooting baskets in front of our

23

house. Some days there was snow on the ground, but I was out there dribbling, shooting, and working on my game.

After school, the team had a two-hour practice. Then I would go home to practice some more. If someone was available for me to play against, that was great, but if no one was there, I would stage a game with some of the all-time basketball greats. My imagination would take me to the lights and glitter of a professional game, and most nights I would be in the position to score the winning basket to lift my team to victory. Almost every time I missed that shot with the imaginary clock running down, I would get fouled, and I would win the game on the free throw line.

My love for the game of basketball and my desire and willingness to dedicate hours to playing it stayed with me even into college. I played for a small college in Northern California, and although the team required only two hours of practice a day, I regularly spent five or six hours in the gym. I usually began the day shooting free throws and working on my ball handling for an hour before my classes. As soon as I was out of class, I would head back to the gym to help the girls' team with their practice. I would run through their drills with them, help their guards work on defense, or just fill in wherever the coach asked me to. After a two-hour girls' practice, I would start right in with my team. Even after our regularly scheduled practice, I would usually stay to play some more.

Looking back at my obsession, I realize now how addicted I was, but back then I didn't notice. Even if I had, I wouldn't have cared. I played because I loved to, and I practiced because I wanted to be good. Some days I didn't feel like getting up early, but I did it anyway. Some days I was tired and wanted to walk through the day, but the end result meant too much to me. Sometimes I had to force myself to play, but I was always glad I did.

Spiritual Laziness

Spiritually we have a choice, just like I did with my practice schedule. We need to decide whether we want our faith to mature, and if we do, then we need to set up a plan to help us get there. Spiritual growth is not merely about remaining close to the mountaintop feelings we sometimes have; spiritual growth is also about establishing some disciplines. It involves practicing until we improve, and then practicing some more.

Just like the days I didn't want to practice basketball, sometimes we don't feel like spending time doing what we have already decided we need to do. We have so many excuses, so many distractions, and so many things that can take up our time. Even when we establish priorities, we sometimes go against them. We must examine the devices that keep us from spending time in spiritual pursuits.

The main issue is, What steals your time? What are the things in your life that pilfer the hours in your day? Do you spend too much time entertaining yourself and not enough time strengthening your faith? If so, you may need to consider the amount of time you spend watching television or listening to music. Does your time disappear as you talk on the telephone? Then you may need to set some personal guidelines if you are going to spend adequate time with the Lord. What about extracurricular activities? Do they consume you? It may sound harsh, but if you are too busy for God, then you need to give up something. Because your most important priority must be to build your relationship with the Lord, you must examine the things that infiltrate your life and steal your time.

When you throw yourself into the pursuit of spiritual growth, you will find that you enjoy the process as well as the end result. Once you talk yourself out of your laziness and your lethargy, the journey is exciting. You won't be disappointed.

I am assuming, since you are reading this book, that you realize your spiritual development is the most important matter that faces you as you mature into an adult. As you look at your life and pinpoint your priorities and what you want to become, you must establish the disciplines that will help you grow.

Practice God's Presence

Your spiritual growth will be determined not by the things you learn or the skills you develop but by the time you spend with the Lord. Any person who spends time in the presence of the Lord will grow in his or her spiritual walk. Conversely, it is impossible for anyone to grow without spending time with God.

David knew how important it was to know the presence of the Lord. Even though he spent many years running from his enemies, David's one request to God was that he could spend time in his presence. *"One thing I ask of the* Lord, *this is what I seek: that I may dwell in the house of* the Lord *all the days of my life, to gaze upon the beauty of the* Lord" (Ps. 27:4, emphasis added).

Think about that. He said, "If I can have only one thing from you, God, I just want to spend time with you. I don't want more wisdom to rule. I don't even want you to wipe out my enemies or promote my name. I just want to be with you."

Exodus 33 tells how Joshua would accompany Moses to the tent of meeting. God would come down and talk to Moses just like a friend would talk to his best friend. After some time, Moses would go back to camp, but Joshua would stay in the presence of the Lord. Joshua's priority was to know God, and he established the discipline to make it happen. Eventually God promoted Joshua, and he led the people of Israel.

Although the need to practice God's presence seems like a difficult command, it is much more than a command. It is an opportunity. If you want to grow, time alone with God is available to you. Practicing his presence is not difficult either. All it takes is for you to make a conscious decision to include God in your life. Making this relationship a priority will take some time and effort on your part, but you are not begging God to do something to which he is opposed. His desire is to join you as you walk through life; he is simply waiting for you to give him entrance. Unless you make the decision to do so, growth will be slow at best.

Following are some ideas of how to practice God's presence. Some of them may work for you, or they may lead you to other ideas of how to incorporate this principle into your life.

Establish a regular time to spend with God. This may sound like a basic principle, but it is foundational to developing intimacy in your relationship with the Lord. Too many people say they are going to spend time with God "whenever I get a chance," and they never do. The morning comes too early, and after an inhaled breakfast, they are out the door for the day. After a hard day at work or school, they come home, and relaxation becomes a priority. Following a few minutes to kick back (which usually turns into a couple of hours), television and phone calls consume their attention. It isn't long before the evening has drifted away. Unable to stay up another minute, they drag themselves off to bed, never taking time to spend with God.

Personally, I believe that every person should set aside a regular time to meet with the Lord, rather than leaving such a meeting to random chance. I have found that mornings are better for me than evenings. I always know when I have to leave the house, but I am never sure what time I will be home or what my plans will be in the evening. If I relied on random chance, my day would be gone before I spent any time with the Lord. My relationship with God means too much for me to go an entire day without that communication.

Whether morning, afternoon, or evening, it is wise for you to set aside some time in your schedule to meet with the Lord. Discipline yourself so that this time becomes a regular meeting. Regularity will not become a rut; rather, it will create stability for your spiritual growth.

Find a place that works for you. Throughout my life, different places have been good places for me to spend time alone with God. When I was in high school, my bedroom was my sanctuary. In college I would park my car, listen to worship music, and read my Bible. When I was a youth pastor in San Jose, the sanctuary of the church was the best place for me to meet with God. Then came our youth room in Colorado. Now, when I am not traveling, I find it easier to concentrate and focus on the Lord when I am alone in my office. When I am on the road, I like to go to restaurants by myself.

Whatever your preferences, find a place that will help you focus as you pray and study God's Word. Such a place needs to be relatively free of distractions so that your mind will not wander. Most young people find that if they retreat to such an environment, they are more able to hear the Lord.

If you are a music listener, begin your day with music that helps you think about God. The style doesn't matter. Perhaps you like contemporary Christian music, or old hymns, or gospel favorites. Whatever the sound, make sure the lyrics are uplifting. Once you get into your day, you may be confronted with social issues, school concerns, or relationship problems. Sometimes the things you face daily do a pretty good job of keeping your focus off the Lord. That is why it is good to begin the day by looking in the right direction. If you walk through the halls at school with an anthem exalting God ringing in your head, you will feel equipped to face whatever the day brings.

Memorize Bible verses. "I have hidden your word in my heart that I might not sin against you" (Ps. 119:11). Memorization is a good way to hide the Word of God in your heart. If you do that, you will find the strength to keep from sinning, while at the same time you will stay in God's presence. I have found that I feel closer to the Lord when I am actively memorizing Bible verses.

When looking to memorize Scripture passages, write them on 3 x 5" cards. In this way, you have made your project portable. You can slip the cards into your back pocket or drop them into your purse. Then you can pull them out anytime you have a spare minute.

Just a couple weeks ago, our ministry team was headed to Nebraska to do a convention. As I was loading our van for the trip, I grabbed some of the 3 x 5″ cards containing Scripture I had been memorizing that week. Throughout the first couple hours of our drive, I kept looking at the verses as I committed them to memory. One of the teenage males who is on our team also memorized them with me.

When memorizing verses, it is good to have a technique in place to review what you have already learned. If you want the verses to stick with you for your entire life, reflect on them every other week or so. If you forget a verse, spend some extra time committing it to memory.

Write down what God is showing you. Journaling is a good way for you to keep track of what God is teaching you. If you write down thoughts that come to you as you read your Bible, you will be able to revisit those thoughts in the future.

One teen used a journal to outline sermons. In her devotional time, she prepared messages with points, illustrations, and Scripture passages. Writing down what God was showing her helped her "preach" great messages to herself. These written notes also helped her when she took a mission trip and needed to share in services overseas.

Taking time to write down your thoughts will help you to think through issues clearly as well as keep a record that you can review. When you put situations into words, you will recognize more clearly how God has been with you, blessing you, answering your prayers, and teaching you. Later as you review your journal entries, you will grow in faith and your trust in the Lord will increase as you realize that he is going to continue to be there for you.

It does not matter how you do it, but you should practice God's presence. Your personality may not fit any of the five suggestions listed above, but if you want to grow with God, you need to spend time with him. How you do it is up to you, but discipline is a necessary component. In God's presence you will find that your *walk* will turn into a *run*.

Principles to Ponder and Practice

- If you are serious about spending time with God, you must set aside a regular time to meet with him. When are you going to meet with God? And for how long each day?
- Where are you going to meet with God?
- Does music help or hurt you as you practice God's presence?
- What do you believe God is asking of you in terms of verse memorization? Set some goals and make memorization a regular part of your spiritual life.
- Begin to journal. Take time to record what you are reading, what you are praying about, and what the Lord is saying to you.

Communication
IS the
Key

Communication
IS the
Key

I want to tell you a story about two people. Let's call them Mike and Anna. They grew up several hundred miles apart, and they never met until Anna was in her late teens. Anna had heard stories about Mike, but every story she had heard made him sound too good to be true. She was not sure he even existed. Mike was also aware of Anna. In fact, they had been in the same room on occasion, but Anna had not recognized him. Although Mike had longed to be introduced to her, they did not formally meet until Anna was a junior in high school.

One summer in early June, Anna was invited to attend a church camp with her friend Stacy. For lack of better things to do, Anna accepted the invitation. After arriving at the campground, Stacy and Anna began to do typical teenage things, running around, having fun. As they sat at the dinner table that night, Anna thought about how glad she was that she had come. She was having a blast. She had needed to escape her home situation for a week, and camp was proving to be the perfect distraction from the tension that was waiting for her at the bottom of the mountain.

Thinking that the camp was all about fun and activities, Anna leaned over and asked Stacy what they were going to do after dinner. Stacy quickly told her that they had to go to chapel. Caught off guard by this information, Anna asked for details. Stacy did her best to describe what the next two hours would be like. "We will sing some songs, and then someone will talk to us."

Wanting more clarification, Anna asked what the speaker would talk about. Stacy didn't have a definite answer, but she mentioned that in the past, love had been one of the themes. This appeased Anna. She had always been intrigued by the concept of love. Quietly she decided chapel might not be all that bad.

As the teenagers piled into the chapel building, Anna chose seats toward the front. As the music began, Anna looked uncomfortable, but she tried to fit in. She wanted to hear about love. Soon the speaker took over, and his topic *was* love. He talked about a love that would overlook all failures. He explained that someone existed who would love them even if they weren't worthy. Anna listened intently.

Soon the evening came to a close. Anna was interested but confused. Who was this person who would love her? With questions ringing in her head, she walked quietly next to Stacy back to their cabin. As they began to climb the stairs, Stacy asked what Anna had thought of the speaker's comments. Not reluctant to voice her opinion, Anna told her friend that she was interested in meeting the person the speaker had talked about.

As a smile broke over Stacy's face, she asked Anna to follow her. A few yards away from the cabin, she asked Anna to sit with her on a large log. Then Stacy began to explain the things the man had spoken about during the chapel service. She asked Anna if she wanted a relationship with the one who would love her always. Shocked at the stupidity of her question, Anna replied, "Of course."

Stacy reached out and grabbed Anna's hand, stood up, and began to walk. Anna was confused but decided to go along. Stacy began to babble about how Anna was really going to like Mike. "He is the perfect friend, and he will always be there for you."

After a short walk, Anna looked up and saw a figure standing a few feet ahead. As she approached, Anna noticed that something was different about him. Something in his eyes was drawing her in. She was about to meet him for the first time, yet something about him convinced her that he had known and cared about her long before this night. Stacy led her right up to him and introduced the two. Instantly, Anna began to share her hurts and concerns with him, and he seemed genuinely to care. It was like no other relationship she had ever had.

The relationship had begun. Mike and Anna were inseparable for the rest of the week. Wherever Anna went, Mike followed. Anna enjoyed herself. She knew she did not deserve a friend like Mike, but at the same time, she wasn't about to give him up. Their conversation flowed like a river rushing over a waterfall. They had so many things to talk about, and Anna wanted Mike to know everything. The more they shared, the closer to him she felt. Before the end of the week was over, they had made a lifelong commitment to each other. Mike and Anna were best friends.

Anna left the campground feeling like a new person. She wanted everyone she knew to meet Mike. Her love for him was overwhelming, and she knew everyone needed a loving friend like Mike.

The intensity of their newfound relationship lasted a month or two, but then things began to change. Nothing was different with Mike; he was still the same. But something was dramatically different with Anna. When she first came home from camp, she was consumed with him—every moment was spent talking to him and taking walks with him. In the beginning she invited him to go everywhere she went, and he was never too busy that he wouldn't accept her invitation. But now she would forget that he wanted to spend time with her. In the morning instead of waking up and calling him to talk about the day ahead, she rolled right out of bed and headed straight for the bathroom. Her morning primping ritual lasted over an hour and took her right up to the time when she had to run off to school. Although Mike waited at the door ready to go with her, Anna had stopped inviting him. A couple of times Mike showed up in one of her classes, but Anna did not notice him. Mike went home wondering why Anna was beginning to ignore him.

After school, cheerleading practice took a couple hours. Mike always watched, but Anna never noticed. She talked to her friends and never saw Mike looking at her, wanting a few moments of her time. Almost every day after practice, Mike would join her family for dinner. Mike sat right next to Anna, but it never helped. Anna didn't feel like talking about her day.

Homework followed dinner. Then TV and the phone. After a bath, Anna climbed into bed, never once thinking to call her best friend. Mike was always waiting by his phone, but Anna neglected him.

On a rare occasion (usually a Sunday), Anna would spend a few hours talking with Mike, and then it would seem as though things were back to normal. But the next day she would forget about him.

One of the saddest things about this situation was that Mike was always willing and wanting to talk to his friend, but she was not. The more time she spent ignoring him, the more independent she became, and the harder it was for them to really communicate even when she wanted to.

One day Anna was having a really bad day, and she turned to talk with Mike. Sitting right next to her, he lovingly listened to all the problems of her day. When she asked for his advice and he responded, she couldn't understand him. It was as if he were mumbling. She got angry with him and thought he was not speaking clearly, but their lack of communication had affected her hearing. He was talking as he always had, but her ears were not working correctly.

This vicious cycle continued for several months. Anna ignored Mike most of the time, yet he was always there waiting patiently. They were still friends, but their relationship was not as strong as it had been or as it could have been. Mike had been true and faithful, but Anna had stopped communicating with Mike, and they had grown apart.

Healthy Communication with God

In any relationship, communication is the key to its health and success. By now you have probably figured out that the story about Mike and Anna is not about a couple of friends. It is about a new Christian and God's love.

I have seen many young people fall in love with the Lord and start a vital and exciting relationship with him only to stop communicating with the Lord. If you stop communicating with God, your relationship with him will become stale, and you will grow apart. One of the main lines of communication with God is prayer. If you talk with God through prayer, your relationship will remain healthy. If you don't, it will suffer. Here are some keys that will help you as you approach your prayer life.

Be Real

As you talk with God, recognize that you are trying to build a relationship with him. You will experience more success if you strive to be yourself. When some people talk to God, they attempt to imitate other Christians, perhaps someone they heard pray in church. They even try to quote that person's sentences and tone. Such an act will not help you as you seek to build your relationship with God.

Instead of pretending to be someone you aren't, put down your mask. Look up at God and talk to him as you would a friend. Don't put on a religious show; be real.

Communicate What You Feel
Before You Tell God What You Want

Prayer is not "The Heaven Shopping Network." Communicating with God is not about demanding new toys and material things. It is about expressing your feelings, concerns, and anxieties to God. When you do, you open yourself up so that he can effectively comfort and encourage you. Only when you express your feelings can he really minister to you.

When you are lonely, tell him. He already knows what you are feeling, but when you share your feelings with him, you are giving him permission to do something about them. Openly share with him when you feel like a failure and are questioning your ability to do what is right. Confess your insecurities. If you make communication a habit, you will begin to change as he deals with issues in your life. Take time daily to tell him how you feel.

Pray about Great Matters

Talk about things that really matter. In your prayer time, pray about your future. Discuss your walk with the Lord. Talk about your hopes and your dreams. Most Christians wait until they reach a crisis before they pray about important matters, but if you pray about them daily, God will give attention to these things in advance, before they break down.

When you pray about your future, God goes ahead and clears the path he has chosen as best for you. When you talk to God about your hopes and dreams, God can shape them. You have also silently given him permission to go ahead of you and make the preparations that need to be made.

I am not implying that you should make demands of God. Rather, as you share with him what is on your heart, you surrender these things to the Lord.

Pray for God's Will

In Matthew 6:10 Jesus taught the disciples to pray, "Your will be done." He modeled this principle also. "Father, if you are willing, take this cup from me; yet not my will, but yours be done" (Luke 22:42).

If you want your communication to be pure, every day you should give God permission to accomplish his will, not yours, in your life. At times you will think you know God's will for your life, but you would be wise to continue to pray for it.

Even though I was convinced that God had brought Mary (my wife) to me, I surrendered our relationship to the Lord until the day I got married. Almost every day of our dating life and engagement, I told the Lord that if he did not want me to be with her, I would call it off. On my wedding day, I talked with God and gave him permission to call it off. I am grateful that he saw my need for someone like Mary. However, had he wanted to take this relationship away from me, I am confident that he would have had a reason. He would have been saving me for something better.

Whenever you pray, "God, accomplish your will, not mine," you are pleasing the Lord. Not only that, but you are positioning yourself to receive his blessing. He cannot bless you when you are holding on to your own desires, but when you want his will, he can give you his best. His best is always better than your best. Trust him even in tough situations. He won't require something from you that he won't replace with something far better.

Stop Talking and Listen

One of the ways God answers prayer is by giving his children specific direction. You may be praying about your future, and God will tell you what college to go to. You may be telling God that you are lonely, and he will remind you that you are loved and never alone.

Communication is always two-way. If you always talk and never listen, you aren't communicating; you are controlling. Take time to listen daily. The longer you serve God and the more time you take to listen to his voice, the more clearly you will hear it.

Leave Your Problems at Jesus' Feet

God desires to take all your pressures from you. In this life, you will experience stress, anxiety, fear, tension, and many other emotions and pressures that will crush you if you let them. When you let God remove them from your shoulders, however, you will sense a freedom and a peace, for you will know that he is taking care of all your problems. "Cast all your anxiety on him because he cares for you" (1 Peter 5:7). Carry everything to Jesus, then unload. And when you turn to leave, don't pick anything up again. He can handle everything you leave at his feet.

A friend of mine wrote a song that has always been an encouragement to me when I am feeling pressure.

When the answers to my questions seem so far away,
I lay it before you.

41

When confusion overwhelms me, O Lord, teach me
     to say,
I lay it before you.
When the weight of situations is more than I can bear,
When I'm lonely or discouraged hear my solitary
     prayer,
I lay it before you.
Lord, here I am, with hands lifted to you.
I'm yielded to your holiness and power.
Open my heart, do what you want to do.
I am yours and yours alone, here's my life, my heart,
     my song,
I lay it before you.

Whenever you pray, lay everything before God—every weight, pressure, and concern. He wants to take them off your shoulders. You can't carry them, but he can.

What Happened to Mike and Anna?

When we last talked about Mike and Anna, their relationship was nonexistent. They weren't communicating, and it was destroying their friendship.

A couple months have passed, and things are starting to look up. Due to some severe circumstances in her life, Anna felt desperate and began to talk to Mike again. She has been spending quality time with him now for two weeks, and she is remembering what made her reach out to him in the beginning. He is such an encouragement to her. Whenever they talk about her struggles, he seems to make everything better. The problems still exist, but after talking to Mike, the weight lifts.

Now that they have been rebuilding their relationship for several days, Anna can even understand Mike again.

He makes sense, and he gives great counsel. Whenever she follows his instructions, things turn out well. She has renewed her commitment to build their friendship and has promised never to neglect her friend again. As long as they keep their lines of communication open, they will have a great relationship.

Principles to Ponder and Practice

- Be real. Take some time today and let your mask down with God. Talk to him about some areas in which you are struggling.
- Instead of only making requests, take some time and tell God how you feel. Talk to him about your insecurities and your fears.
- Pray about great matters. Pray about the future not only the present.
- Pray for God's will. Ask him to accomplish his purpose in your life.
- Take time to listen for God's voice. Ask him some questions that you have been pondering and take time to listen. Hearing God's voice is a skill that anyone can master but one that must be practiced.
- Make a conscious effort to give all your stress, questioning, and fears to the Lord in your prayer time. Then leave them at Jesus' feet.

Is the Bible Important?

The Bible has gotten a bad rap over the years. I have heard many teenagers say that the Bible is boring and that it doesn't pertain to their lives. If they knew exactly what the Bible contained in its pages, however, they would crave it. It contains stories of war, love, and encouragement. It tells about people who did incredible deeds and lived fantastic lives. It contains poetry, history, and futuristic stories. It is the most exciting book ever written.

What I love best about the Bible is not what is written in its pages, however, but what it does when I let its words saturate my heart. There is a supernatural component to the Bible that I can't explain but have experienced. It helps me shape my life into what God wants it to be.

Even though I believe the Bible is worth reading because of what I can learn, it does something on an invisible plane that is even more exciting. God's Word gets past my head and touches my heart. It renews my mind and silently equips me with what I need to live for God. It takes God's heart and his character and begins to reproduce them in my life.

No One Saw My Problems

I have come to realize that there are two types of people in the world: those whose problems are visible to everyone around them and those who hide their problems very well. Some people openly struggle, and some struggle silently and privately. Although the first type of person receives the most press and attention, the people in the second category have to fight to overcome their failures as well. Many times, however, they are frustrated because they aren't making progress.

I was the second type of person. Although I was the model Christian on the outside, I knew my failures and recognized my hypocrisy. I would cringe every time someone would compliment me on my maturity or character, because when I looked in the mirror, I didn't see my polished mask. I saw the corruption attached to my life.

Although I grew up in a Christian home and was in church a minimum of three times a week, I struggled with some major issues in my life. To other people they might not have seemed major, but to me they were paralyzing. I battled daily with my mind, my mouth, and an addictive habit of stealing.

Even though I wanted to serve God, my mind was corrupt. I had difficulty looking at females in a pure way because of how my mind was working against me. I tried to convince myself to think in an appropriate manner, but no matter how many pep talks I gave myself, I couldn't control my thoughts. It was as if they were controlling me.

My mouth was another problem. I could not seem to tell the truth. I lied, exaggerated, and made up stories all day long. Soon I reached a point where I lost track of reality. I was unsure of what was true on certain issues because I was such a good liar; the truth was blurred even in my mind.

My final problem, yet the one that bothered me the most, was my stealing. I did not steal once in a while; I stole every day. I knew God did not want me to steal, but I couldn't seem to stop. Whether at school, in a store, or at home, I would find something to take.

These three problems were overwhelming. I did not like the way I thought, the way I talked, or the way I acted. My inability to overcome these three areas caused me to dislike myself. I would sit on my bed at night and rebuke myself for being so weak. I would beg God to forgive me for falling again, all the time wondering when he was going to give up on me. I didn't know how to overcome my problems. I couldn't control them; they controlled me. I was desperate!

Then it happened. My world began to fall apart when my parents saw my struggles. Although I didn't like who I was, it was easier to deal with my problems when I could hide them. I thought I would get a handle on them someday, but with each passing day they seemed to get worse instead of better. My parents began to catch me in lies, and one day they caught me stealing. They were confused, hurt, and scared. Because they had never had to deal with these parenting dilemmas before, they were in search of an answer. They decided I should meet with the youth pastor at my church. Hopefully Frank could figure me out and talk some sense into me.

I remember that Friday night. My encounter with Frank was held before an activity night at our church. My mom dropped me off, and I found him in his office. As I began to explain my problems and that I felt I could not control them, I could tell he didn't know quite what to say.

After listening attentively for several minutes, however, Frank began to talk. He told me that I did not have a stealing problem or a lying problem. He told me that I had a heart problem. As he talked I began to understand that the things I saw as my problems weren't; they were just the symptoms of my problem. My real problem was my heart.

After Frank changed my perspective, he then began to address the root of my difficulties. He said, "Sean, I can tell you only one thing that will change your heart." He paused for just a minute before he went on. "If you want your heart to become purer, you must let God help you. You must begin to read your Bible. If you spend time with God every day by reading your Bible and praying, God will change your heart."

As I sat across the desk from him, I didn't think it would work. He was telling me that if I read my Bible every day, I would stop stealing, my mouth would clean up, and so would my mind. I didn't believe him. I had read the Bible

48

before, and it had been boring. Many times when I had read it, I had walked away confused. At times it just didn't make sense. However, I was in a desperate state. I wanted to overcome my problems, and my pep talks and self-rebuke sessions had not been effective. I was willing to try Frank's methods, and I told him I would.

Right there, Frank took out a piece of paper and wrote down a plan. I agreed to read two chapters from the New Testament before I went to school and two chapters from the Old Testament before I went to bed at night. I made a commitment to read at least four chapters every day.

As we were about to leave our meeting and get ready for our evening of fun, he looked at me very sincerely and said, "Sean, if you want to change, I believe this will help you. But you are the one who has to read. I can't do it for you."

That day marked a change in my life. From that day on, I began to read the Bible twice a day. I wrote down what I read and gave a list to Frank every couple weeks. However, I wasn't doing this for Frank; I was doing it for me.

I don't recall when my actions began to change; all I know is they did. A couple months down the road, I looked back and realized I hadn't stolen anything for several weeks. I recognized a change in my thought life and in the control I had over my mouth.

I really believe that as I read the Bible on a regular basis, God changed my heart and mind. He helped me overcome the things I could not overcome by my own strength. At the time I did not understand how it had happened, but God has taught me some things since then. Let me show you what the Bible will do if you let its words saturate your heart.

Taking the Sword out of Its Sheath

"For the word of God is living and active. Sharper than any double-edged sword, it penetrates even to dividing soul and spirit, joints and marrow; it judges the thoughts and attitudes of the heart" (Heb. 4:12). This verse clarifies how the Word of God works. The Word of God:

> is living and active. There is movement to the Word of God. It does not remain on the pages when it is read; rather, it jumps off and proceeds to bring change and healing to areas affected by sin and unaffected by the Lord's touch. When something is alive, there is movement. This is the case with the Word of God.

> is sharp. There is a sharpness to the Word that is meant to cut. The power of the Word of God is able to sever ungodly attachments. It can bring freedom from addictions and problems when nothing else has helped.

> is able to penetrate beyond the surface. It can move past the exterior and go down deep. Instead of dealing with surface issues, it can move into the recesses of the spirit and soul. People may not be able to see beyond your mask, but the Word of God can find the root of your faith or problems.

> judges the thoughts and attitudes of the heart. Once it has moved toward the heart issues, it exposes, sifts, analyzes, and judges the thoughts, purposes, attitudes, and motives that exist there.

This is what happened to me. When I began to read the Bible on a daily basis, I took the sword of the Spirit out of its sheath and gave it permission to change me.

As soon as I made a commitment to read the Word of God, I noticed movement. Although some days I didn't draw specific application from what I read, the Word bounced around in my being. It moved and affected everything it touched in my life.

The more faithful I was in spending time reading the Bible, the more the Word began to go deeper in my life. No one had seen the calluses on my heart, but the Word wasn't fooled by my mask. My defenses could not keep out the penetrating, energized, and operative Word that was released as I read.

Finally, it judged the thoughts and attitudes that were attached to my heart. The Word that I had sown saw at least three things clinging to my heart: an impure thought life, an out-of-control mouth, and a propensity to steal. At once, it judged these things as inappropriate for my life, and then it began to do battle.

The sharp sword of God began to take chunks out of the problems I had wrapped around my heart. Over the course of time, I began to feel more freedom. As I saturated my heart with God's Word, I dropped my problems and addictions. Although I still have to use discipline and battle to remain pure in all these areas, they do not control me anymore. I have found victory over these things that used to victimize me. How? The mighty sword of the Spirit came and cleansed my heart.

Making Bible Study a Priority

I believe you now understand that the Word of God has incredible significance and will benefit your life if you make it a part of your life. However, you may need some help concerning how to begin. Here are some practical tips that will help you as you seek to make Bible study a priority in your devotional life.

Establish a regular time to read the Bible. I knew I was going to spend time reading the Bible every morning before school and every night before I went to bed. It soon became a habit in my life, one that I looked forward to. If you are going to be faithful in building this spiritual discipline, you must establish a regular time and stick to it as best you can.

Establish a goal of how much you will read on a daily basis. Although you don't want to anchor yourself to an unattainable goal, you want to stretch yourself in this area. Ask the Lord to help you as you establish some goals. Get out of your comfort zone, but don't bury yourself under an unrealistic expectation.

Decide where you will begin reading. I strongly recommend that you establish a plan for reading Scripture. Do not randomly open, point, and read. Decide ahead of time where you want to start, and then have some continuity to your reading. You could start in Matthew, Mark, Luke, or John if you want to become more acquainted with the character, attitudes, and deeds of Christ. If you want to read about how God can use ordinary people who are committed to reckless acts of faith, read Acts. Are you trying to build more intimacy with God? Then read Psalms. Read the two books of Timothy if you want to see how God instructs a young leader.

Before you open your Bible, pray and ask God to explain the passages you will read. Although I have explained that you don't need to understand everything in Scripture for it to change you, if you do understand, the Bible is working on two fronts. Ask God to reveal to you his will and his heart as you read. Before you open the Bible, bow your head and take on a teachable attitude.

Write down what God shows you. As you begin to read, move slowly enough to let God teach you. Read with a pen or marker in your hand. Keep a notebook close by so that as God shows you things, you can record them for future study or reflection.

Find an accountability partner. It is wise to have an accountability partner who will walk with you through the regular struggles of your life. Where Bible reading is concerned, it is also good to have a friend you can share with and who will remind you of the commitments you have made. If you know your friend is going to ask you if you are still spending time reading the Word of God, you might be encouraged to stay on track.

Memorize Scripture verses. By committing Scripture to memory, you are storing up weapons against the enemy. Your sword becomes transportable. Whether you are in a line at the movies, in a car, or have a spare moment at school, the Word that is hidden in your heart can come out and encourage you. It will give you a defensive weapon against the enemy's attacks and an offensive weapon to help you mature in your faith.

Pray for application. Every time you finish reading, stop and ask God to help you apply the truths you have just encountered. As you begin to understand what God is trying to tell you through Scripture, your life will conform to his will. Tell God you need his strength to make it happen. That is a prayer request he is eager to answer.

A Tree That Produces Fruit

If you meditate and dwell on God's Word day and night, you will yield fruit. If you want to live with godly character and attitudes, you must delight yourself in the Word.

Blessed is the man
>who does not walk in the counsel of the wicked
or stand in the way of sinners
>or sit in the seat of mockers.
But his delight is in the law of the LORD,
>and on his law he meditates day and night.
He is like a tree planted by streams of water,
>which yields its fruit in season
and whose leaf does not wither.
>Whatever he does prospers.

PSALM 1:1–3

Principles to Ponder and Practice

- What do you like best about Scripture? What do you like the least?
- Are there any problems in your life that you would like to overcome? Are these things heart problems? Do you think that by saturating your heart with Scripture God could give you victory?
- Using the eight points listed toward the end of this chapter, come up with a workable strategy for reading the Bible. Make a plan of attack so that you know how you are going to devour the Word of God.
- Record in a journal what you read and what you learn.

Worship Will Change Who You Are

Different Approaches to Worship

On a snowy day in February, I contemplated the young people I was working with. I thought of Amber, a sixteen-year-old girl from my group who had no spiritual support at home. Her parents had never attended church with her. She attended a public school, and none of her close friends were Christians. Looking at her life, you would assume she would not be able to live for the Lord. Because she was attractive and a cheerleader, there was no end to the amount of pressure she felt to sell out her convictions. Yet one thing kept her going. She loved to worship.

She would walk into our youth meetings and instantly lift up her heart to the Lord. Many times she would not sit with her youth group friends because she wanted to focus her attention solely on the Lord. When she was worshiping, you could see in her eyes the joy, hope, and encouragement she longed for. Only when she was worshiping did she seem happy and content. She longed for those times of worship. It was her only escape from the struggle of life.

Then I thought of Jenny, another case of someone who felt isolated, especially spiritually. Her parents were divorced, and she had never had a strong father figure. She felt as though she had no real friends, and she had never had a boyfriend, which weighed heavy on her heart. Many times she wondered if she were good enough. Although everyone else saw her strengths, she saw only her weaknesses. Only one activity helped her look past her failures: looking into the face of Jesus.

Whenever Jenny had the opportunity to worship the Lord, she would. She did not care if the worship team sounded good, was in tune, or even sang the right words. Jenny recognized an opportunity to be intimate with the one who accepted her. Like Amber, she escaped the problems of her life by getting lost in the arms of the one who had promised her eternal life.

Although Joel knew Amber and Jenny, he was entirely different. His family was solid. He did not deal with insecurity; rather, he dealt with pride. He was an excellent athlete who started two varsity sports when he was a freshman. He knew he was important, but he was a little confused as to why. It is difficult not to be impressed with yourself when everyone is telling you how great you are. You would deal with pride too if you had as many females flirting with you as he did. Yet when it came down to it, Joel was not sure if he was loveable. If he got in an accident and could not play another game, he wondered who would be there wanting to be his friend. If he suddenly lost his good looks and charm, would he still feel important? It was a vicious cycle, and it was something he dealt with on a daily basis.

When Joel surrendered to the presence of God through worship, however, he was able to regain perspective as to why he was important. He remembered in those times that it was not because of what he could do, who liked him, or how popular he was. He realized he was important because of who loved him. Every week, it was a visible transformation. Joel the jock walked into the youth room, but when worship began, he turned into Joel the little kid, captivated by the one who loved him.

Sarah went to a Christian school and had a better support system than the other three. If you looked at her life, you would think she had it all together. No looming problems. Her parents were solid. They loved each other and they loved her. She was in church twice a week. She got good grades. She was competitive at everything she participated in. Her report card wasn't bad, and her social calendar was pretty full.

One day when I was in the chapel at the school Sarah attended, I was getting ready to speak to her student body. Looking around the room, I realized one other thing about Sarah that was different from the other three. She did not love to worship. She did not get lost in an intimate moment with the Lord when she had the chance. As a matter of fact, she seemed bored during worship.

Looking around, I noticed that everyone in her row was the same. Sure they were singing the songs, but the blank stares and their body language communicated clearly that they were not enjoying it, nor were they getting anything out of it. Continuing to glance around the room, I noticed that boredom was the normal response. Young people who were truly worshiping were the exception.

Something inside me wanted to jump up and rebuke these young people. I thought to myself that they were missing an incredible opportunity. They were singing, but they weren't worshiping. They weren't receiving encouragement and joy. They were missing out on the hope and comfort that God wanted to bring to them. Why was this the case?

I understood that in their school they had a worship service every morning. The same team led the worship times every day, and the songs were the same. Yet I was still slightly upset. I began to think of all the young people in my group who would have loved the opportunity to start off their day at school with fifteen minutes of worship. What focus that would have brought to their day. I thought of Joel, Amber, and Jenny. I knew they would not have wasted that opportunity. I pictured them standing in the room with their hearts raised to the Lord, smiles on their faces. They would not have been bored with this worship service; they would have drawn strength from it.

Many people sitting in churches do not understand what worship really is and what it can do in their lives. If they did, they would long for more opportunities to worship.

What Worship Is *Not!*

Worship has not been achieved when you sing a song that talks about the Lord. You can pull a heathen in off the street and throw the words to a beautiful song up on the overhead. He can join you in reciting the words, but that does not mean he is worshiping.

Worship is not about the feeling you get in a group but what you offer to the Lord as an individual. Although I love great worship services and enjoy the energy that is created when many people worship as one, worship really takes place in the hearts of individuals. It does not matter where a person is or what is going on in the room. There may be sweet music, or it may be in math class, but when someone focuses his or her heart on God, worship takes place.

Worship has nothing to do with your body. Although you may attend a church in which members demonstratively worship the Lord through raising their hands or kneeling, worship is about what you do with your heart, not your body. There have been times in my life when I was in church and I was not happy. Instead of ditching my bad attitude so I could focus on the Lord, I played the game. I knew what to do so that everyone would think I was worshiping. Although I was raising my hand and singing a song, my heart was not thinking about the Lord. I was not worshiping; I was pretending.

What Worship Is

Worship takes place when a heart is focused on the Lord. When you let the things that usually consume your thoughts fade away so you can look upon the Lord, you are worshiping. When you see God as all-powerful, you are worshiping. When you sit in a room and feel incredibly loved by your Creator, you are worshiping.

Although you are looking up at him, he usually distributes incredible gifts to you when you worship him.

Sometimes worship fills you with joy. Sometimes hope. Always love. Never condemnation. God will speak to you when you take time to worship him. He will give you direction, perspective, and strength.

When you focus on him, you will see things as they really are. Your problems will not look overwhelming, your mountains will not look immovable, and your dreams will seem within reach.

Your Perspective Changes When You Worship God

God speaks to me in the craziest ways. When I was moving from California to Colorado in the fall of 1989, I had a weird experience that taught me an incredible truth.

Riding in my rented Ryder truck, I was bored. There was no radio and no one to talk to. After several hours on the road, I was beginning to zone out. It was all I could do to keep my attention on Interstate 80. Just as I was leaving Elko, Nevada, a bird flew in front of my truck. In what seemed like slow motion, I saw this bird look at me and smile. Then he tilted his body toward me, revealing his belly, and dropped the largest amount of bird doo-doo that I have ever seen. Direct hit! My windshield and the entire grill and hood of my truck were whitewashed.

It was such a strange experience that I immediately began to laugh. Turning on the windshield wipers, I tried to clean off the mess. The wipers only smeared it and kept pushing the chunky liquid across my glass. I was having trouble seeing because of it. That is when God decided to teach me an incredible truth using this strategically placed visual aid.

For the next two miles, I began to notice that I only saw what I looked at. When I looked at the mess on my window,

I could not see the road. When I looked at the road, I could barely see the mess in front of me. Lovingly God began to show me how easy I was to distract. My focus (my road) should always be Christ, yet all it took was a little problem in my life to distract me. I began to think of times when I was so concerned about my future that I forgot to look at the road. I should have been pursuing God, yet I had spent so much time looking at the unimportant distractions that I had become consumed with them and had neglected what was really important.

When you spend all your time concerned with your problems (family problems, relationship problems, concerns about your future, injustices that you face), they seem to consume you. Many times they look too big to conquer. Yet when you focus your attention on God, all your problems come into focus. You realize how small your concerns are in light of how big your God is.

Worship provides a good balance. If you are consumed with issues that you face and you feel hopeless, you need to worship the Lord. Your problems will not go away, but they will be less intimidating.

An Obligation and an Opportunity

I believe that every Christian has an obligation to worship. It is something that God requires of us. It is part of the reason why we have been chosen. "But you are a chosen people, a royal priesthood, a holy nation, a people belonging to God, that you may declare the praises of him who called you out of darkness into his marvelous light" (1 Peter 2:9).

Worship is a responsibility, but it is also an opportunity to usher in God's presence. When we worship (focus our attention on God), the experience changes us. We begin to see the true balance of things (God is huge and nothing else compares), and we encounter hope.

The Bible says that God gives grace (help/assistance/ unmerited favor) to the humble (dependent). If you want to receive help from God, you only need to recognize that you need him. When you worship and you see how small you are compared to God, you can't help but feel inadequate. In that moment, God sees your need and moves to assist you.

You should never try to manipulate God, but if you need help, start by worshiping God. Don't miss an opportunity to have God fight your battle. Don't be so prideful that you don't let him guard your reputation. Look to him, and he will be your shield, your armor, and he will fight for you. Don't forget, he never loses.

Myth: "I Can Only Worship When…"

Although it is much easier to be led in worship, it is possible to worship God even when you are alone. Not only is it possible, if you are going to stand for the Lord, you *must* learn to worship in solitude.

David was one of the greatest worshipers the world has ever known. He wrote the majority of the psalms, the first original worship book. Although he was an incredible worshiper, the Bible records very few times when he worshiped in public. Most of his times of worship took place when he was alone.

I believe David learned to worship when he was a shepherd. I picture David sitting on a rock with his harp. With his sheep gathered around, he would sing to the Lord. He was not performing, he was allowing his music to express his heart for and devotion to the Lord. David had a worshiper's heart even before Samuel anointed him king as a young man. He had made a habit of worshiping God in private even before he took down Goliath. His moments of worship put the world in perspective and gave him the ability to fight against the odds. And he worshiped while he was alone.

You must learn to worship God daily if you want to stand for him. Use worship tapes, read the psalms aloud, or take a few minutes to vocalize how incredible God is. Whatever you do, do something. If you want to be known as a man or woman of God, you must worship him. If you want to be used by God, you must focus your attention on him. You must learn, as David did, that before you can stand in public, you must worship in private.

Principles to Ponder and Practice

- Which of the four students (Amber, Jenny, Joel, or Sarah) mentioned in this chapter do you most relate to? Why?
- Make worship a priority in your life. For the next week, spend at least ten minutes worshiping the Lord each day.
- Have you ever had your perspective changed through worship? Record the story.

It's Time to Grow Up!

As you develop your commitment to Christ, your faith will either grow strong as you mature or grow old through the routine of your faith. God wants your faith to mature, but he doesn't want it to grow old. He wants your spiritual life to remain exciting, fun, and vital. He wants your faith to grow every day out of an intimate relationship with him.

However, if your faith just grows old, it will become stale and boring. Its vitality will disappear as its routine increases. Rules and regulations will guide your faith to a slow death.

As Christians, we must commit ourselves to a mature faith. We cannot be satisfied with less.

Maturity Is More Than a Destination

Although maturity is a goal we set our sights on and strive for, it is also a direction and a perspective. We will never reach a point at which our faith has reached the pinnacle of growth. We will never become completely seasoned. We must always work for and walk toward maturity.

Even if you are young in your faith, you can still make mature choices. You can set your course toward spiritual development. You can have a mature outlook on life. For that purpose, let's consider the components of maturity and mature people.

Maturity Is Found in Your Responses Not in Your Circumstances

Many of the things that are recorded about Joseph's life in the Book of Genesis are clouded in adversity and difficulty. He was sold by his brothers into slavery. He ended up in a foreign country far from his family. He was taken advantage of and then accused of a crime he did not commit. Yet while in jail, he kept pure motives and served with a good attitude. His circumstances were not pleasant, but his response was mature. What was done to him or what happened around him did not define his life. He chose to relate to his life in a positive way.

Mature people are not dominated by their surroundings and their circumstances. They find the ability to rise above the negative situations in their lives and hold on to God with a sense of purpose and destiny.

Maturity Is Not Measured by How Much You Know but by How Much You Apply What You Know

The Pharisees were well educated. They knew God's laws and were quick to let people know how well versed they were. They wanted to look mature by debating the ins and outs of the law, but they did not apply the principles that they knew so well—at least not internally.

God's command to us is clear. According to James 1:22, we are to do what the Word of God says. Although memorization and study are good disciplines to practice, they do not make you mature. Application not information is what the mature person seeks.

Maturity Is Not Found in Comparison with Other People but Is Recognized in Personal Progress

Immature people love to compare themselves with people who are in a less favorable position. They think that if they can point out how far along they are in their journey compared to someone else, God will overlook their mistakes. Some people use this comparison as an excuse to stop striving for God's best.

Mature people realize there is always more room for growth and that the journey they are on is an individual one. They set goals for personal growth and evaluate themselves based on their own progress.

Mature People Neglect the Easy Way in Favor of the Right Way

Many immature Christians look for the easy way in life. They go along with the flow rather than create waves. In many cases, however, the easy way is the wrong way. Mature people do not take the easy road; they opt for the right one.

The pressure of the world buries immature people, but strong Christians find the ability to get out from under it and climb above it. Pressure is not as crippling to mature Christians because they care more about doing the right thing and pleasing God than doing the easy thing and pleasing people. Sometimes the strength of their convictions makes the choice easy, but at times the choice is difficult. Even in the midst of difficulty, however, mature people find a way to do what they know in their heart is right and will please God.

Mature People Deal with Their Lying Feelings So They Are Able to Act on Truth That Never Changes

Because we are human, we have strong feelings. Many times our negative feelings of hopelessness, anxiety, and sadness try to overpower us. Even mature people have strong feelings and emotions. However, people rooted in the truth of God realize that if they feel hopeless, that feeling is a lie. If God is with you, there is always hope. Some people allow their intense feelings to paralyze them with inactivity, causing their spiritual convictions to lie dormant, but mature people have figured out how to deal with their feelings without letting them become paralyzing. They find a way to cast all their cares on the Lord, because he promises to carry them.

Mature people recognize their feelings. They can separate them from reality, and they refuse to be crippled by them. They do not allow their feelings to influence them to give up or quit fighting. Mature people know how to stay focused on what they know instead of how they feel.

Mature People Let God In

It happened just last week. I was speaking at a Christian school for five days. Feeling out the crowd, I made some observations. A group of people in this school thought they were the leaders. They had a very high opinion of themselves socially and spiritually. They thought they were mature. As the week progressed, however, it became obvious they were not.

Their posture and their attitudes convinced me that they were not willing to let God in. They had reached a plateau in their spiritual life and didn't want to continue to grow. With every ounce of energy they had, they were fighting with God. They refused to allow God to shape them in any way.

Mature people run to God not from him. They embrace his conviction in their lives, even if it is difficult. Because they realize that his correction always leads to fruit produced in their lives, they give him open access to any area he chooses to touch. Mature Christians invite God to work in their lives.

> Search me, O God, and know my heart;
>   test me and know my anxious thoughts.
> See if there is any offensive way in me,
>   and lead me in the way everlasting.
>
> PSALM 139:23–24

The More Mature You Are, the Fewer Masks You Will Wear

Immature people try to hide their weaknesses. Mature people recognize that it is in their weaknesses that God is strong. The people who are ashamed of their imperfections walk in pride trying to protect their images and their reputations. Mature Christians realize that it is not their responsibility to look good or to protect themselves.

The letters Paul wrote to encourage the early churches make up the majority of the New Testament, but Paul did not hide his faults. On the contrary, he bragged about them (2 Cor. 12:7–10). He shared openly about the misdeeds in his past (1 Tim. 1:16). He talked freely about his current struggles (Rom. 7:15–20). Why would anyone admit to multitudes of people that he was far from perfect? There is only one answer. He knew that God accepted him even though he was messed up but that God wasn't going to let him stay that way. He also recognized that by being transparent with his shortcomings, such openness would give others hope that with God's help they could overcome theirs.

By hiding behind masks, many Christians slow their ability to overcome their faults. Their purpose in hiding is to keep others out, but it also does two other things. It keeps God out, and it keeps the real person hidden. By intentionally running from people, they end up staying away from God (the only one who can bring about the change that is needed), and they prevent the people they are trying to become from ever entering the scene.

Mature people let down their masks because they want to be seen for who they are. They are God's workmanship. Even though they are not perfect, God is partnering with them to bring about positive changes.

Mature People Are Never Content

I don't care how much you know about God, there is always more to know. No matter how many years you walk with him or how intimate your relationship becomes, there is still more of him to be revealed and more of you that needs to be changed. Mature people realize they need to continue to grow.

The more people experience the Lord, the more time they want to spend with him. His presence is addicting. Mature people don't want just a sip; they want to take a drink from the hydrant. When they bring one meeting with God to a close, they can't wait for the next one.

Immature people are content and complacent. They take just enough to keep them feeling good about themselves, and they base their faith on rules, routine, and obligation. They don't realize that a vital relationship should exist. No wonder they do just enough. Mature Christians, however, keep coming back for more.

The Choice Is Yours

The difference between mature people and immature people is found in the fruit their lives produce. Many people want to take shortcuts to maturity, but there are none. Maturity is a day-by-day choice to go in the right direction.

Some people want to be *perceived* as mature. They don't care about mature character or faith, only about having the appearance of maturity. The mask goes on and the act begins. If people are not mature but want to be considered mature, they will strive to do mature things, but they will neglect the process of growing in maturity. They seek the approval of people, many times directly disobeying the Lord's mandate and will for their lives.

I am not trying to convince you that you need to be mature. I believe you already want that for yourself. Nor am I trying to shame you into maturity. What I am attempting to do is give you permission to be what you want to be. I am trying to enable you to see what maturity is and choose that road for yourself. If you choose maturity, the fruit of your life will be abundant. Your relationship with God will be vital and always growing, and you will allow God access into every corner of your life.

Principles to Ponder and Practice

- How do you respond to difficult circumstances in your life? Is this something you need the Lord to help you with?

- On a scale of 1 to 10, how well do you apply what you already know about God's will for your life? Write down three areas that you are going to work on.

- Do you find yourself comparing yourself to others instead of keeping an eye on your own faith journey? Take some time and write down two things in your spiritual life that have improved over the past year.

- What are the feelings or emotions you deal with the most? How often are they contrary to what God says and expects of you? What are some practical ways you can overcome that problem?

- Do you ever shut down when God is trying to speak to you through a service, book, or speaker? Make a commitment that you will not allow that to happen to you.

- Do you ever feel the need to wear masks? How often do you hide behind a facade because you are ashamed of your imperfections? Pray and ask God to help you overcome this habit of hiding.

- One day I found myself praying these words: "Lord, I want more of you, but I never want to have enough of you." Mature people want more, but they will never be content. Take a moment and tell God never to let you grow content in your relationship with him.

Dealing with Famished feelings

When I was growing up, I did not understand how to read the Old Testament. I liked the stories, but I often couldn't grasp the meaning of what was written there. Because I felt the first thirty-nine books of the Bible were nothing more than a strange storybook, I avoided reading them.

While in college, I learned a method that helped me understand how to approach the Old Testament. Whenever I read stories in the Old Testament, I began trying to locate three things:

1. man's nature
2. the devil's schemes
3. God's character

By learning what to look for, the Old Testament came alive to me. As I applied this simple principle, I became fascinated with this part of Scripture, and God began to teach me many things. I began to understand that every story in Scripture contains at least two of these three elements. At times I have to look a little deeper, but at least two of them are always there. Sometimes I can find all three.

Let me give you an example. Genesis 25 gives us an early account of Jacob and Esau.

> Once when Jacob was cooking some stew, Esau came in from the open country, famished. He said to Jacob, "Quick, let me have some of that red stew! I'm famished." . . .
>
> Jacob replied, "First sell me your birthright."
>
> "Look, I am about to die," Esau said. "What good is the birthright to me?"
>
> But Jacob said, "Swear to me first." So he swore an oath to him, selling his birthright to Jacob.
>
> Then Jacob gave Esau some bread and some lentil stew. He ate and drank, and then got up and left.
>
> So Esau despised his birthright.
>
> VERSES 29–34

This is a weird exchange, even among brothers. However, one day rather than reading over this passage quickly, I asked the Lord to show me what man's nature is. What can I learn from this passage that will help me overcome my tendencies to fall into Satan's traps?

As I prayed, my eyes began to rest on the word *famished*. Esau came in from the open country famished. I needed to understand what that word means and how the concept affects my life. When someone is famished, they have an "intense and desperate feeling of being unfulfilled." Esau came in with an intense and desperate feeling of hunger. It was so incredibly strong that he thought he might die.

Although you may never be so hungry that you think you are going to die, you probably know what it is like to be famished. The majority of the people in this world are intimately acquainted with "intense and desperate feelings." I don't doubt that you know these kinds of feelings. If you don't learn how to respond to them, however, they will control you and steer your life. If you allow God to teach you how to deal with your famished feelings, you can choose your own paths.

A Famished World

Although at one time or another the majority of people have famished feelings, they come in many different areas of life and in varied strength. I am not arrogant enough to think that I can list all the areas in which people struggle, but I have listed a few.

- *Loneliness.* Many people in the world today know intense and desperate feelings of loneliness. Typically these people never let anyone see their anguish about feeling alone, but they are haunted by such feelings. After having spent hours with some of their best friends, they pull away into the solitude of their bedrooms to wonder if anyone cares. Though people surround them, they still feel alone.

- *Insecurity.* Some people feel as though they never measure up and never fit in. They feel like outcasts and misfits. Often they don't know how to talk to anyone about their feelings, so they suffer in silence.

- *Pain.* Many people in this world are crippled by pain. They have known abuse, rejection, abandonment, and loss in their lives. Their feelings are intense and desperate. They don't know if they can ever deal with the memories or overcome the injustices that have been done to them. Although statistics say there are many who can relate to their pain, they feel as if no one can.

- *Meaninglessness.* A high percentage of young people deal with feelings of meaninglessness. They want to make a difference, but they are not sure if they will. They want to live a purposeful life, leaving behind a positive legacy, yet feel they won't. Some feel as if they are the only person ever born who is destined to live an insignificant life.

- *Hopelessness.* Our world is hopeless without Christ, and that hopelessness has reached out and grabbed hold of many hearts. Even some Christians have lost all hope of being able to walk with God, overcome habits, or succeed in life. This hopelessness brings depression to some and steals energy to try from others.

- *Fear.* People today are crippled with fear. They are scared of people, society, and solitude. They are afraid of being alone, but they are also afraid of being around people. Fear has a grip on their lives, and it leaves them feeling powerless and weary. Their intense and desperate feelings of fear keep them from trusting God and taking steps toward him.

The devil plays on that part of our human nature that lets our emotions get out of control. He twists the truth and distorts the facts so effectively that we forget to run to God. Instead, we go for the quick fix.

The Quick Fix

Esau went for the quick fix. Do you see the devil's strategies and schemes in this story? The devil stationed a temporary and costly solution in the path of the famished Esau. Esau came in from the open country and encountered his brother cooking up a storm. Esau got a whiff of that stew and about went crazy. "Quick! Give me some of that."

The devil will always offer you a worldly answer. It will look good and smell good, but it will not be good. Many times in our famished states, however, we are not able to discern what is good and what is not. Rather than seek God's answer to our problems, we stop at the quick fix. Esau did just that, and Jacob was more than willing to appease him, as long as Esau gave him something in return. "First sell me your birthright."

There are three things you need to recognize when you have intense and desperate feelings:

1. There will always be a quick fix close by.
2. It will always cost you something.
3. It will never meet your need long-term.

Esau saw a quick fix waiting, but it was going to cost him his birthright, his inheritance, his place as firstborn in the family, and what made him unique. The food would also be gone soon. It would not last. But he was famished, and he sold something very precious for something worth very little.

If Esau had been in his right mind when the sale was suggested, Esau would have laughed and walked on past Jacob. But his intense feelings did not allow him to think logically and clearly. "Look, what good is my birthright to me if I die?" Esau's need to bring a resolution to his famished feelings forced him into the corner of incorrect thinking.

This same thing happens all the time today. "What good is my virginity to me if I am lonely?" "What good are my convictions to me if I am the outcast?" "What good is my sobriety if I am hurting?" So many excuses, yet the same theme. I have intense and desperate feelings, and nothing matters except taking care of them. This kind of thinking is where the problem lies.

Where Is God's Character in All of This?

Man's nature is to have famished feelings and to stop at a quick fix. The devil is always ready to offer an immediate answer to our pain. Two problems: The devil's answer costs us something, and it never lasts.

Where is God in all of this? Let's look at Genesis 25:28, which says, "Isaac loved Esau." I am convinced that if Esau would have been able to say no to the quick fix, he would have found his dad in the tent just a few yards off ready to meet his need. His father loved him and never would have let him go hungry. He would have offered him anything he had at no cost to his son. Why? Because Isaac loved Esau.

God will do the same for you. God deeply cares about your intense and desperate feelings, and he wants to see you walk in peace and joy. He will offer you everything he has to meet your needs and help calm the storm of your emotions.

If you are lonely, he will spend time with you and let you know you are never alone. If you feel as though you just don't fit in, he will convince you that he accepts you and is proud of you. He will speak to you about the incredible and strategic plans he has for your life. You may feel as though you don't count, but he is counting on you. Hopeless? Not after you spend some time with him.

The problem is that we have a tendency to do what Esau did. We stop at the quick fix instead of running into our Father's tent and telling him that we need him. God is there waiting for us to maneuver around the devil's answer to get to him. Not only will God offer a better solution, but it won't cost us anything and it will last forever. Remember, in John 4, Jesus told the woman at the well that if he gave her water she would never thirst again.

You Must Deal with Your Famished Feelings

Many people think they do not have to deal with their intense and desperate feelings. As a Christian who wants to walk with God intimately and fulfill God's plan for your life, however, you must. Extreme emotions have been the downfall of many Christians. Either they neglected their feelings, deciding not to deal with them, or they didn't recognize how those feelings drew them to ungodly means of fulfillment.

If you want God to help you overcome famished feelings, he will, but you must come to him as a child in need of your Father's care. Begin now by recognizing the ways that famished feelings control your thoughts. Decide now not to stop at the quick fix, but to go instead to find your Father.

Principles to Ponder and Practice

- What are the three things you need to look for when reading the Old Testament?
- What are some intense and desperate feelings you deal with?
- When do you deal with them the most?
- The devil will always offer you a quick fix. List the two negative things that are present in his offer.
- Do you recognize the devil's quick fixes? Name some that you have accepted.
- Are you going to make a commitment to go into God's presence when you are feeling famished? How are you going to do that?

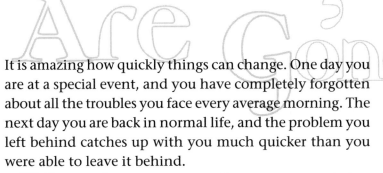

What to Do When the Feelings Are Gone

It is amazing how quickly things can change. One day you are at a special event, and you have completely forgotten about all the troubles you face every average morning. The next day you are back in normal life, and the problem you left behind catches up with you much quicker than you were able to leave it behind.

While attending a camp or conference or on a mission trip, you don't think about what awaits you when you return. You are too busy hanging out with your friends, feeling the tangible presence of the Lord, and letting God speak to you, as well as speak through you. Then in a few short hours, everything seems to be back to normal. Your life returns to the way it was. The tension that could be felt between your parents is still there when you return home. Homework still awaits you in a large pile on your dresser. Those lies that had been spread about you at school are still circulating, and with each day you were gone, it seems as though another couple people began to believe them.

Within hours of walking through your door, you get a phone call from one of your friends. You are invited to a party. You know you should not attend this kind of party, but you are still tempted. Finding the courage to do what you know is right, although not in the right way, you make up an excuse about being busy and hang up the phone.

Sitting in the chair by your bed, you are disgusted with yourself, not because you did something wrong but because a part of you wanted to. Your thoughts begin, *I can't believe I almost told him I would go. Did these past couple days mean nothing to me? I thought I was different. Evidently I was wrong.* With your head buried in your hands, you ask a question: "Why was it so much easier to serve God last week than it is today?"

Mountaintop Experiences

Although it was a rhetorical question and you did not expect an answer, I believe you deserve one. Understanding why it is so much more difficult to live for God at home than when you are away may help you as you try to build your convictions so you are able to stand against temptation wherever you are.

Anticipation and Expectancy

Most young people who attend a camp, conference, youth rally, or go on a mission trip come with a different attitude than they normally have at home. Even if they are regular church attendees, they show up at the special event with a sense of excitement about what is going to take place. They may be anticipating a great time in the presence of God, or they may feel the large crowd is exciting. Whatever the reason, they have come with an excitement that God can use to get through to them. If the attitude is one of expectation, there is a good chance they will receive something.

A man used to sit by the temple gate called Beautiful. Being crippled from birth, he was needy. Unable to get himself to the gate each morning, he had to be carried. Day after day, this man sat by the gate and asked for money. One day he had an encounter with Peter and John. As they walked past him, he asked for money. Stopping in front of the man, the disciples looked toward him. Noticing that they were looking toward him, he "gave them his attention, expecting to get something from them" (Acts 3:5). The man thought he was going to receive some money, but instead he received a touch from the Lord. God healed him. He went home different from the way he had been when he came.

When young people attend special events, many times they have a similar experience. The day begins like an ordinary day, but something changes. Their anticipation begins to build. It may be due to the atmosphere of the event, or it may be ushered in with worship. The expectancy that they "will get something" opens the door for the Holy Spirit to get past their mask and tough exterior. When the Holy Spirit finds fertile soil, the Lord touches them. Things begin to change. The things that had been troubling them for years seem to fall away and are forgotten.

Bring It Home

I believe one of the signs of spiritual maturity is when you can hear and respond to the Lord's voice as he speaks to you even when no one else is around. When you don't need a preacher or a full worship band to get you prepped to receive, you will grow quickly. God desires to speak to you every day. Train yourself to look at him with anticipation. Like a child looking into her father's eyes wondering what gift he has stored for her in his briefcase, look at your heavenly Father, knowing that he has something special in store for you every day.

Aggressive Unified Prayer

I would never imply that church members do not pray for their weekly services, but I will venture to say that more people pray about special events. These prayers fuel the fight in the spiritual realm. This battle that is fought in prayer pushes back the darkness and ushers in the presence of the Lord. When teenagers walk into a room that is saturated with the presence of God, chances are they will receive from the Lord.

In Acts, a story of miraculous intervention is recorded. Peter was in a dungeon between two soldiers, and he was bound with two chains. He was sleeping, but the church was *earnestly* praying. Suddenly a light shone in the cell, and an angel woke up Peter and told him to get his things; he was leaving. The chains fell off, the doors opened up, and the soldiers never woke up. After Peter and the angel had walked into town, Peter said, "Now I know without a doubt that the Lord sent his angel and rescued me from Herod's clutches and from everything the Jewish people were anticipating" (Acts 12:11). After Peter realized what had taken place, he went to the place where the people were praying and told them the story.

The point is that people were praying, and Peter was delivered. The Bible doesn't declare that Peter expected to be set free. All we know is that outside parties were praying. They knew that Peter needed some help. He didn't even realize what was taking place until it had already happened.

When you attend a camp, you can be sure that the people organizing the camp have been praying about it for months. If your parents are godly, they have been praying that God will meet you there. While you are gone, they are praying for you as well. When people see the camp announcement in the church bulletin, be assured that several people are silently volunteering to lift up the camp in prayer.

When there is this much unity and specific direction in prayer, the event and the individuals who are attending will be affected. Be assured that one of the reasons God seems to lovingly confront you and challenge you at every camp and conference you attend is because of the prayers that are being lifted up to heaven.

Bring It Home

You would be wise to implement this principle in your daily walk with God if you want to grow. I am not suggesting that you put a flyer in your church bulletin recruiting people to pray for you. However, I do think that everyone should have three to five people pray for him or her daily. Think of the people who care the most about you, and ask them to pray for you each and every day. Volunteer information that gives them specific direction as they pray for you. In return, promise to pray for them.

There Are Fewer Distractions in Your Life

In your everyday life, many things fight for your attention—television, friends, the radio, and so many other things. These things steal time and attention from your relationship with God. Although you will never find a place where you are totally isolated from such distractions, many times a week or a weekend designated to spiritual growth offers fewer of them and helps you focus on other things. Surprisingly enough, this small change in the pattern of the way you spend your time can bring about great results.

Bring It Home

If you want the impact of a spiritual event to last, try giving up some of these items. Some young people have found that if they cut back on their phone conversations, they have one less distraction that competes with their spiritual life.

One teen went home from a youth convention and put a note on her television set. It read, "Read and pray; don't forget God today." She used that note to remind her not to let the business of the day steal her time with the Lord. She made a decision that she would not watch television unless she had spent time with the Lord that day.

If you are going to give up some of your time on the phone or in front of the television, you must use that time wisely. If you take your TV time and use it to go to a movie instead, your spiritual life will not be benefited. Likewise, if you give up your phone time and end up spending that hour at the mall with your friends, your objective was not met. If the Lord leads you to give up something that is taking up your time, spend that time with the Lord and invest in your relationship with him.

Worship Is Easy

When you wake up Tuesday morning and are getting ready to go to school, how much do you think about God? Are you reminded every Wednesday morning before your first class that God loves you and wants to walk with you throughout the day? If you are like most teenagers, you probably don't think about such things.

When you are at a special ministry event, however, you are confronted every day with the fact that God is there. Chances are, several times a day you are encouraged to worship, to think about the Lord's love and greatness. In such a setting it is easy to remember who God is and how you feel about him.

Worship is easy at these events. I am not talking about the act of worship (when a guy gets up with a guitar and leads you in song). I am talking about the heart of worship (when you are consumed with gratefulness, awe, and love for the Lord). Worship is not about repeating someone else's words; it is about seeing God for who he is. It is about having a proper perspective. When the good things of God are continually pointed out to you, it is easy to worship. When you are conscious of his activity in your life, worship just happens.

Bring It Home

Can you have this same worship encounter as you are getting ready for school? Can you experience God even while you are in class, surrounded by students and a teacher who do not want to worship with you? Absolutely, but you must remind yourself of God's greatness and glory, because no one else is going to. If you make a solid decision to start off each day focusing on the Lord and his desire to walk with you, you can have a heart of worship even when it is difficult.

The Word Is Changing You

I know you saw this one coming, but it is true. The reason you grow more quickly at special events is that you are being saturated with the Word of God. The speakers are spending several hours educating your spirit.

A principle applies here: "I have hidden your word in my heart that I might not sin against you" (Ps. 119:11). The Word of God, when taken into your life (whether by choice or accident), challenges the sin and the evil in your life. You grow because the Word outbattles the sinful nature.

I can look back at my life and identify different spiritual seasons. There were times when I struggled with my thought life or other areas of sin, and there were also times when those things didn't seem to have as tight a hold on me. As I look back over those times, I can find parallels between the time I was spending with God and what was happening with me. When I was spending adequate time reading my Bible, I was walking in victory. When I was neglecting my quiet times and not spending time in the Word, I was struggling.

Bring It Home

Saturate yourself. When you let the Word get deep into your spirit, you will see a difference. The principle applies whether you are at camp, on a mission trip or retreat, at a conference—or at home.

It's Gone; Can I Get It Back?

If you have lost your intense feelings for God, I want to tell you that you can get them back. God never intended for you to lose them, and I hope you are beginning to understand where they went. They did not stay behind in the room where you met, and they did not leave when the speaker went home. What changed was the way you approached God. If you want to get the feelings back, read over the last five points again and begin to make the necessary changes.

At the same time, however, although this chapter talks about the "feelings" you had at the special event, you can never believe your emotions. Your emotions will lie to you whenever you give them the chance. Let me explain. The Bible clearly says that God will never walk away from you. "Never will I leave you; never will I forsake you" (Heb. 13:5). However, you probably have felt as though he was not close to you. So is the Bible wrong, or are your feelings wrong? It doesn't matter what you feel like. If God said he is right there, then he is. You can't always believe your feelings.

Rather than trying to keep the feelings, concentrate on keeping the commitments you made. It doesn't matter what you feel like, but if you let your convictions and your commitments slip, you do have a problem.

Your commitment should always be to grow and never fall away.

Principles to Ponder and Practice

- What changes did you notice in yourself when you attended a special activity in the past?

- Have you ever felt as though God were not near you? Do you believe he left your side?

- Are there certain times when your feelings tend to lie to you more than others? When and about what?

- Anticipation and expectancy. Make a commitment to hunger for God. Before you enter a church or youth service, ask the Lord to speak to you. Then listen.

- Aggressive unified prayer. This week approach three to five people and ask them to pray for you on a daily basis.

- There are fewer distractions in your life. Choose one thing that takes up several hours of your time every week and trim back on that activity for thirty minutes every day this week. Spend that time building your relationship with the Lord.

- Worship is easy. Every day this week begin your day with worship. Spend time reflecting on God's greatness. Thank him outloud for his goodness to you.

- The Word is changing you. Make a commitment to devote some time each day to reading your Bible.

10

Barriers that Prevent Growth

In my ten-plus years of youth ministry, one question has always loomed in my mind. As I look at the teenagers I have been called to shepherd and pastor, almost in anguish and frustration I keep asking, "Why aren't some of them growing?" So many of the young people I see in my church and who participate in youth services are not growing spiritually. Although they attend church and are confronted with principles that are supposed to assist in their spiritual development, they are making very little progress, if any at all.

The problem is not specific to my youth ministry; it is a problem that affects many of the young people who participate in youth ministries all over the nation. I believe there are many reasons why teenagers are not growing, but I will focus on seven.

Seven Reasons Why Christian Teens Don't Grow Spiritually

1. Laziness

Laziness promotes inactivity. If there is no activity in your spiritual life, then there will be no growth. If a student does not make time to spend with the Lord because he or she enjoys sleep or relaxation too much, that person will not grow.

A small percentage of teens value spending time with God. Instead, most value entertainment. After all, watching television takes less effort and initiative than going into your bedroom, closing the door, and spending some time in prayer or Bible study.

I am not saying that students are lazy in general. Actually, they have great amounts of energy, which they often spend on activities they consider fun. However, many students are simply too inactive when it comes to spiritual matters. They neglect their Bibles, and their prayer lives are minimal. Many are frustrated with their lack of spiritual development, yet much of the time it can be traced to their own refusal to take the time and pay the price to grow spiritually.

2. Pride

They were some of my favorite youth group kids. They would stop on a regular basis and see me at the office, many times bringing me something sweet to eat. They almost never forgot to say thank you when I took the youth group on an outing, and they even remembered my birthday. They loved the Lord, and they appreciated their youth pastor. This group of friends came to our prayer meetings, and they almost never missed a youth service. They were faithful, and for the first year or so, they grew spiritually. Their growth was obvious in their attitudes and in their actions. They were making progress.

I am not sure when I began to notice the disturbing trend, but something began to change in their lives. After a while they stopped listening to the people who spoke in Sunday school or youth group. It was almost as if they listened for the first five minutes, figured out what the topic was going to be, and then rolled their eyes in disgust as they decided they didn't need help in that area. Pride had entered their lives, and it was altering their walk with the Lord. Something had convinced them that they were "mature" and that they had arrived. I am not sure why they thought they had learned everything there was to know, but their actions and attitudes declared that they were not interested in learning more or maturing further.

They became less faithful in their attendance of prayer meetings and youth services. When they did show up, they no longer came to learn; they came to perform. In the past they had come to prayer meetings to receive from the Lord; now they came to pray so everyone would notice how much they knew and how eloquent they were. Instead of attending youth group to spend time in the Lord's presence, they acted as if they were there to do the other teenagers a favor.

As you can imagine, the change scared me, but it is typical of what pride does. When pride enters the scene, people stop focusing on God and begin to look at themselves. When this happens, growth stops, stagnation begins, and this is followed by the deterioration of their relationship with God.

Spiritual pride is difficult to define and difficult to detect. It is amazing to me that some people who have the most pride in their lives do not see it, while on the other hand, some people who are very humble continually ask the Lord to strip them of their pride. Instead of giving a verbal definition of what pride is, I would like to talk about what pride is not. The opposite of pride is humility, and where there is humility, pride does not exist.

A correct biblical definition of humility is, needy or dependent, particularly or specifically on God. When pride comes in, we lose sight of the fact that we are not self-sufficient; we need God. Pride convinces us that we do not need to hunger after the Lord, nor do we need to wait on him. As a result, we begin to depend on ourselves. What we know or what we can do becomes enough. Instead of spending time with the Lord because we want to remain close to him, many times prideful people read their Bibles so they can gain head knowledge with which to impress people.

When pride comes, dependency on God leaves. One of the quickest ways to stop spiritual growth is to become content with where we are. Pride stops movement. "A man's pride brings him low, but a man of lowly spirit gains honor" (Prov. 29:23).

3. Focus on Others Rather Than on God

How many times have people sat in a church service as the minister preached a message, only to ignore what God was saying to them because they were wishing someone else had been there? "Man, I wish Sue would have been here. She really needed to hear this." Sometimes we lose our focus as we look down the row, hoping that our neighbor is paying attention. When we get involved in any of these church games, we allow the enemy to distract us from what God wants to teach us.

Every time we enter church, or open our Bible, or consciously take time to spend with the Lord, we should ask him to speak to us. Whether he chooses to reveal our weaknesses so that he can strengthen them, or whether he wants to speak to us about our choices or our future, we should be excited about the opportunity to hear from the Lord. Unfortunately, we often aren't. We would rather ponder someone else's struggles and failures instead of our own. While at times we do so out of godly concern, we often do so out of envy or bitterness. Whatever the reason, we cannot allow it to distract our focus from our relationship with the Lord.

Not long ago I was talking with someone who attends a Christian high school in Denver. I asked him how he was doing spiritually. Almost in a depressed tone he told me that he was not doing great. When I asked him why, he began to tell me about situations and the spiritual climate at his school. He told me that one of his friends was dating a girl who was "experienced," and he was worried that his friend was going to get into trouble. He told me that the girls in his school were always backbiting and gossiping. He told me that the school administration was messed up, and they had no clue what was really going on in their school.

After listening to him for a few minutes, I began to tell him that his focus should not be on others but on his own walk with the Lord. He agreed. He knew he was not concentrating on his own growth; he was looking over everyone else's shoulders wishing they would grow.

The Bible talks about looking at your brother and ignoring your own situation. "Why do you look at the speck of sawdust in your brother's eye and pay no attention to the plank in your own eye?" (Matt. 7:3). This verse is not saying that your problems are always going to be bigger than the problems of the people around you. It is saying that you should not concern yourself with the sins of other people; your main concern should be with the sins you face. You should deal with the things that keep you from growing spiritually rather than dealing with the same issues in someone else's life.

Although you should remain loving and compassionate, you should not be obsessed with other people. When you have an opportunity to hear from the Lord, you should do so for yourself. If you keep your focus right, you will grow, but it is difficult to walk the narrow path when your eyes are always looking at someone else.

4. Lack of Responsibility

Characteristically, babies are dependent. They are unable to feed themselves, think for themselves, or protect themselves. They are needy. They cannot survive without their parents to look after them or someone to assist them with the simplest of tasks. It is impossible for them to take responsibility for themselves.

Unfortunately, the world contains some spiritual babies. It is not that these people are unable to take care of themselves; they have just chosen not to do so. They refuse to feed themselves, think for themselves, and protect themselves. They have chosen to defer these responsibilities to their pastors, youth pastors, parents, and other people they feel are their spiritual guardians. Although they feel as though they are growing, they have really hit a plateau.

Although many young people have reached a point at which they no longer need to be spiritually dependent on someone else, they have not taken responsibility for their own faith life. They would rather have someone else tell them what the Word of God says than study it themselves. The Bible says that some should be teachers, but some teens have not moved away from needing to be taught.

> In fact, though by this time you ought to be teachers, you need someone to teach you the elementary truths of God's word all over again. You need milk, not solid food! Anyone who lives on milk, being still an infant, is not acquainted with the teaching about righteousness. But solid food is for the mature, who by constant use have trained themselves to distinguish good from evil.
>
> HEBREWS 5:12–14

Few things encourage me more than seeing someone grow quickly. Mindy had not been a Christian for long when she realized she could devour the Word on her own. She didn't need to ask permission, she just needed to pick up her Bible and nourish herself. Within a couple months of being saved, she was memorizing Scripture and understanding biblical principles better than many of the young people who had been attending my church for years. She was growing faster than most Christians will ever grow. Why? Because she had so much to learn? Possibly, but also because she learned early on that she is supposed to take responsibility for her own spiritual development.

Many Christian teenagers do not understand that they are responsible for the condition of their spiritual life.

Without knowing it, they blame either their youth group or their church if they do not see spiritual growth in their life. Although God gave pastors and churches to assist you in your spiritual development, they cannot become your only means of nourishment, or you will dry up and wither away. As you continue to grow, more and more of your nourishment must come as you feed yourself.

I am not saying that you will reach a point at which you should remove yourself from spiritual authority and stop listening to men and women of God. I am saying that you need to balance the teaching of others with your own disciplines.

5. Pain

I cannot imagine having to face the rejection and pain that some teenagers have to face today, but the fact is, no amount of pain should prevent you from growing and developing. Young people today are bombarded with family lives that produce hurt, situations in their schools that fuel their insecurities, and everyday events that steal hope. Although these situations are a reality, God is bigger than any of these circumstances.

If pain were a good excuse, Jesus would have chosen not to pursue God's plan for his life. When the first piece of skin was ripped from his back, he would have cried out, "It hurts too much; I give up." When the first drop of blood dropped off his head as the crown of thorns broke his skin, he would have run away. If rejection were a good excuse, he would have called down angels when the people mocked him or Peter denied him. But Jesus knew that pain was not a good excuse. God called him to walk a path, and no pain or persecution was going to keep him from fulfilling his call.

If it were enough to remain true to your convictions only when it is easy, Daniel would have stopped praying as soon as he heard that he would be thrown to the lions if he continued. Shadrach, Meshach, and Abednego would have bowed when the trumpets sounded. But they knew they had no reason at all to abandon what they believed.

When teenagers look back on their lives and their pain, they sometimes blame their lack of progress on their tough life or the persecution they faced. No excuse is good enough for God. Things may hurt, but they cannot prevent your growth and development. Only you can do that.

6. Boredom

When boredom sets in, people stop growing. If teenagers get to a point at which their faith isn't fresh and exciting but stale and old, they neglect the disciplines that fuel their spiritual development.

I met her in the cafeteria on the first day. Looking into her eyes, I could tell she wasn't impressed with me or with the camp. Taking a shot in the dark, I said, "You don't want to be here, do you?" She responded by telling me that her parents had made her come. After a few more minutes of talking, she told me that she was a Christian and had been for many years. She was morally sound. She didn't drink, do drugs, or go to parties, and she was still a virgin. Confronting the fact that she seemed proud of these facts, I asked her why. Almost surprised at my question, she told me it was because the Bible said she needed to live this way.

At that answer, I finally knew how to approach her. I asked her, "Is that all that there is to Christianity—rules and regulations?" She quickly answered, "No," but when

I asked her what else there was, she wasn't as quick to respond. After stumbling over her thoughts for a few minutes, she couldn't answer me. She did not know what else there was to her faith. Uncomfortably, she squirmed in her chair until an opportunity came for her to leave our table. Very politely she excused herself and headed out the door.

For the next three days I watched her and prayed that God would get through to her, and he seemed to do just that. She began to enter into worship, and with each passing service, she listened more intently. The altar call came the last night, and she came forward. I was so excited, I rushed over to her and prayed for her. God was reaching her.

After the service, she waited for me. When I had finished talking to everyone and praying for everyone who wanted prayer, she came up to me and said, "Thanks." She told me that Christianity had always been boring to her. It was always, "Do this, and do that," but this week she had begun to understand that it's not boring. Her walk with God is supposed to be exciting as she gets to know God and lets him teach her how to live. Without me asking her again, she answered the question that she could not answer in the cafeteria that first day. "There is more to my faith than rules; now I have a relationship."

The reason our faith sometimes becomes boring is that we focus on something other than our relationship with God, which energizes our faith. When we are involved in a vital relationship with our exciting God, we can't be bored.

If you associate boredom with your faith, get your focus back on God and begin to pursue building that relationship. It will prevent boredom and allow you to begin growing again.

7. Steady Diet of Spiritual Junk Food

In this country, I see a growing trend toward healthy eating. Even some of the young people I spend time with are becoming concerned about their eating habits, not because of their weight, but because they want to keep their bodies healthy.

Teens would do well to apply the same principle to their spiritual life. When they realize that eating sugar affects their energy and productivity, they should also realize that what they put into their spirits does the same thing. Teenagers are living on a steady diet of spiritual junk food, and it is killing their desire to grow spiritually. They entertain themselves with music, movies, television, concerts, magazines, and books that are not healthy for their spirits; on the contrary, they have a poisoning influence. They need to realize how much these things affect their lives and go on a spiritual diet.

I am not trying to be legalistic; I am trying to be realistic. I am not opposed to the media, but I do want to alert you to three types of influences found in the media.

1. Influences that are positive.
2. Influences that are neither positive nor negative.
3. Influences that are negative.

I made a decision when I was a teenager that I wanted my music to have a positive influence on me. I knew some music would conflict with my convictions and be a strain on my faith, and I didn't want exposure to that. I also knew some music would be neutral—not good, not bad, just there. I chose to spend most of my time listening to music with a positive influence, and I really believe it helped me grow spiritually.

Just as unhealthy food can rot your body, an unhealthy spiritual diet can rot your soul and keep you from growing. When you say you want to grow spiritually yet you don't monitor what you listen to, watch, and read, you are dealing with conflicting influences in your life. If the bad influences oppose the good and outweigh them, you will encounter problems as you seek to grow.

Be Alert

The Bible warns us to be alert (1 Peter 5:8). We are supposed to evaluate our situations and recognize what tactics the devil is trying to use to slow us down or get us off track. If you look at your life and are not pleased with the amount of growth that is taking place, look over the seven items discussed above. Ask the Holy Spirit to help you evaluate your life, to see if one or more of these items is affecting you. If you see any of them slowing you down, begin to combat them with God's help. To ignore them means to let them continue their influence on you. To deal with them means you can get back on the road to growth.

Principles to Ponder and Practice

Do any of the barriers mentioned above affect your life? If you recognize any of these barriers, how are you going to work to eliminate them?

- Are you lazy?
- Are you filled with pride?
- Do you focus on others rather than on God?

- Do you take responsibility for your spiritual growth?
- Do you allow pain to become an excuse?
- Does boredom keep you from pursuing God?
- Do you spend too much time consuming spiritual junk food?
- Are there any barriers to growth in your life that were not mentioned in this chapter?

The Missing Ingredient

"God, there is a generation down there that is crying out for more of you. What are you going to do about it?" The angel had just returned from assignment on earth. Being moved by what he saw, he boldly asked God if he was going to intervene.

"What would you like me to do that I have not yet done? I have given them everything I am. Everything at my disposal is available. There is nothing that I have withheld."

Then God changed his tone. "Come over here and I will show you."

God led the angel over to another area that was set up like a kitchen. Gesturing, he encouraged the angel to look around. "What is all of this?" the angel asked.

"This is my recipe to bring revival and renewal to the earth." Pointing to a large container, he continued. "That is what I am creating. That is what I am doing with this generation."

Curiously, the angel walked over to the container and looked in. He said, "What did you put in here, God?"

"Everything."

"Did you give them grace?" When God nodded, he continued. "Is it enough?"

God responded, "It is more than enough."

"God, this generation is hurting. They need comfort and peace."

"It is in there. All of it."

The angel asked, "What else is in there?"

"I told you that I gave them everything they need. I gave them mercy, healing, my presence, and my power. I have anointed their leaders, I have dwelt in the midst of their worship, and I have been faithful to fulfill my promises." As the angel looked on in amazement, God paused. His mood became somber as he continued speaking. "However, there is one thing that is missing, one thing that makes it all work. This last ingredient is what truly revives the soul and changes lives eternally."

By now, the angel was curious. "What? What is the one thing you haven't given them yet?"

"This ingredient I do not supply. It is something they must give me. The missing ingredient is hunger."

Hunger Is Rising

If you look in Scripture, you will find promises that are activated by hunger. Hunger moves the hand of God. If we are hungry and thirsty, we will be filled (Matt. 5:6). If we crave the Word, we will become mature (1 Peter 2:2). When our hunger pushes us close to God, he will come near to us (James 4:8).

For too long we have been passionless in our pursuit of God. A generation exists that hungers after many things, but God has become a low priority. But that is changing. Hunger is rising. Young people are fasting on a weekly basis asking God to show up. Youth groups are experiencing record attendance at their prayer gatherings. Instead of simply waiting for the next large youth event, teenagers are inviting God's presence into their bedrooms, cars, and schools. They are not content with hearing about what God did years ago. They are begging him to reveal himself again. And he is.

Good Intentions Are Sometimes Not Enough

Last week I spoke at a retreat in Michigan. After one of the services, a young woman approached me with tears running down her face. She told me that she was never going to go back to being the average apathetic Christian she was when she arrived at the retreat. She told me she was a new person.

I really appreciate hearing from people who are passionate about the commitments they have made before the Lord. However, I know that many good intentions are not lived out. Many people make decisions at services and mean them just as much as this young woman, but not all people are able to stand behind their decisions.

People come to ministry events and leave changed. They take their old life, their old problems, and their stale boring relationship with Christ and kill them right there on the altar. In exchange for their old life, they pick up a new one, one that is vivacious and exciting, one that is built on the concept of a growing and radical relationship with Christ. They return home with a precious new life, leaving their old one at the campground.

Over the years I have also seen some disturbing transformations take place in some of these young people after they have returned home. As their camp experience fades in their memory, the person they used to be becomes more a part of their life. The tendencies and habits they thought they left behind at the campground come back to snuff out their new commitments and convictions. The part of them they killed comes back to life.

The Nail in the Coffin

We must learn to put the final nail in the coffin when God changes our lives. We must make such an intense decision to lay aside the old and run with the new that we do not allow the old to creep back into our lives. But how? One of the earliest questions that Christians have asked is, "How do I live by my convictions, resisting the pressure to give in?" Paul, who wrote the majority of the New Testament, even battled with this dilemma (Rom. 7:15–20).

The missing ingredient is hunger showing itself in tangible ways. If you are hungry for God, it will be expressed in action. Hunger is the hammer, and determination is the nail.

As you seek to walk with God, there will be opportunities for you to fall away from your good intentions. You will have to make daily choices that will determine whether you continue to live in the freedom of your newfound life with Christ or face bondage to your resurrected old ways. Hunger for God and his best for you need to outweigh your desire to let your old self creep back in. However, your desire cannot be defined as hunger unless determination is mixed with it.

There must come a day when you absolutely say yes to God and no to the other offers you face. Your heart must be filled with a determination that allows you to walk away from temptation, a determination that will not allow you to be apathetic or coast through life without taking time to meet with God and let him change you. At times you must grit your teeth and decide that you are going to live for God even though it won't be easy.

If you find that hunger inside and it expresses itself through determination, the coffin is finally closed. You are able to live free from who you were, and you are free to pursue who you can be in Christ.

You don't have to be the best educated, the most talented, or have been serving God for many years. If you give God your hunger, he will work in your life. You can stand on the mountaintop of your relationship with God and say, "I am here to stay!"

Points to Ponder and Practice

- What is your hunger level? How do you intend to improve it?
- Hunger is recognizable through your actions. How are you going to live out your convictions?
- You can be the type of person you want to be. Take a moment and write down a statement about your sincere and passionate commitment to growth. Begin with the words, "I choose . . ."

For a free newsletter and a list of materials from Champion Ministries or for information on having Sean Dunn minister at your church, conference, retreat, camp, school, or other ministry group, please contact the ministry at:

Sean Dunn
c/o Champion Ministries
P.O. Box 1323
Castle Rock, CO 80104
303-660-3582